SIMPLE GIFTS

Judy Brown

Order this book online at www.trafford.com
or email orders@trafford.com

Most Trafford titles are also available at major online book retailers.

Printed in the United States of America.

ISBN: 978-1-4669-0392-0 (sc)
ISBN: 978-1-4669-0391-3 (hc)

Library of Congress Control Number: 2011960293

Trafford rev. 12/02/2011

www.trafford.com

North America & International
toll-free: 1 888 232 4444 (USA & Canada)
phone: 250 383 6864 • fax: 812 355 4082

Welcome and appreciation

This collection of poetry is a sharing of simple gifts. Almost twenty years ago, when the first of my poems popped up on a journal page—that odd shift from prose to poetry—I thought it an aberration. But in the years since, poems jotted on journal pages, grocery slips, post-its, and Amtrak napkins, have come to serve as a presence, a guide, a way for me to pay attention to life.

Readers may recognize a poem here and there from collections published informally over the years and circulated among friends and colleagues. The chapter heads echo the names of those earlier collections. And you may see a familiar poem from a poetry anthology or an earlier books of mine.

This collection of "simple gifts" reflects, to me, the honest ups and downs of life, the joys and sorrows, the power of people, place and the natural world. And this collection of simple gifts is dedicated to my husband David, without whose appreciation, stewardship and dedication, this collection would have remained simply a pile of loose poems on the office shelf.

Judy Brown
West River, Maryland 2011

Table of contents

Welcome and appreciation 3
Table of contents 4

Little Bits from Jottings

Perfection 18
No seed grows 19
It is the small space 20
Because you have no money 21
Everybody counts 22
To sit simply 23
Each day dawns 24
A reservoir within 25
I wonder 26
The beauty of the broken 27
Difficult 28
Spring 29
Promise 30
Miracle 31
Courage 32
Mystery 33
Downpour 34
Seasons 35
Surprise 36

Logs 37
Tapestry 38
Winter 39
Lean Years 40
Autumn 41
Transition 42
Leaf 43
Grieving 44
Turning point 45
Maturity 46
Waves 47
Pelican 48
Magic 49
Heart 50
Human 51
Spirit 52

Simple Gifts

Sweet gifts 54
Wolf song 58
Voyager 60
Wanting 62
Knots 64
Proud 67

Carnations 70
Poetry again 73
Beyond 75
Grace 76
Presence 78
Christmas 80
Snow song 82
Dusting of snow 83
I cannot know 84
Sitting on the fence 85
The Pelican 87
They brought new life 89
I write my way 91
There is a turning point 92
Jungle birds 94
The weight of work undone 95
Winter kite 97
Here I am 99
My soul votes no 101
Falling apart 103
Grandma Moses talking with Ed Murrow 104
The barns have all burned 106
Two days from solstice 108
For Dickens
–we thought we had picked you out 109
Surrender 111
Urban Libraries 112
Snow days 114

Wanting II 116

Montana Poems

Vast sky 118
Geese 119
The storm 121
Flash floods 123
Waves on Deep Bay 124
Seeing complexity 126
Dawn storm 128
Webs 130
Hummingbirds asleep 131
A sense of place 132

Courage

Bells 134
Courage II 135
Lace candlelight 137
Moments open 138
Traps 139
Snow 140
Moved 142
Calling 143

Healing 145
Needed 147
Invitation 149
Courage II 151
Arms 153
Feelings 156
Chair 158
Cries 161
Cathedral 163
Alone 165
Dreamed 167
If you were sick 169
Being 173
Lone seagull 174

Island in the Center of the Heart

Wilderness within 176
Longing II 178
Wind 180
Seasons II 181
He asked me 184
Solitude II 187
Time 190
Ceremonies 192
Feather 194

Circles 197
Blue Heron 199
The other way 200
Current 204
Rainbows 205

Labyrinth

Labyrinth 208
Stuck 209
Crocuses 211
Changing 214
Wall 216
Forgiveness 219
Morning Glory 222
Prayer 223
Moonlight in Michigan 225
Sugar 228
Poet's heart 231

All who Wander

Rebirth 234
Recluse 236
All who wander are not lost 237

I've grown lazy 238
I don't know what I am doing 239
Summer sabbatical 241
Rabbit sneeze 242
Rabbit sneezes and bird safety 244
Ten thousand years ago 247
Budget resolution 249
Eaglet 251
The universe 253
Too soon 255
Watching geese 256

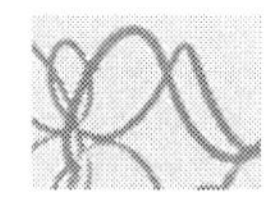

Connections

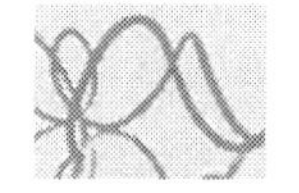

Cornstalks 258
Quilts and carvings 259
Water's edge 261
Awake 264
Center 266
Bullet points 267
Not here 269
Sleeping child 272
Strangers 274
Daughter 276
Granite 277
Hymns 279
Now II 282

Wind II 283
Turning point II 284

Roger's House

Rascals 288
Trilliums 289
Connection 290
Leonardo 292
It doesn't matter 293
Swissair flight 111 295
Time's elastic 297
Truth 299
Thunder 300
India 301
A mourning 304
Miracles II 307
Songbird 308
Dense 309
Synchronicity 310
Moment 312
A deer 313

A Leaders Guide to Reflective Practice

Wooden Boats 316
Fire (original version) 318
Stepping back 320
Life dictates 321
Trust equals speed 323
Things as they are 325
Tad Mule 327
Cynicism in the workplace 328
Trough 329
Ethics is wrestling 331
Occupation 332
Cirque du Soleil 333
Seed 335
There are countries 337
The bridge with a sign 338
Good Samaritan 339
Life's not a battle 340
Competitor 341
Applewood 342
The circles of our conversation 344
Dialogue and measurement 345
Stop it 346
Seconds 348

A thin film 351
Loon song 352
Lunch with Alice 353
Stories 354
Trust 355
The pizza came 357
Some days 358

Sea at Grace Bay

Barefooted 360
Infinite encounters 361
Nothing's more active than the sea 362
The Hat 363
Shards 364
Hospitable 365
Twenty-eight poems 366
The lessons 367
The ocean waves 368
The tide is coming in 369
Why are we led here? 370
The shells stand for all things 371
No one swims alone 372
Caught in the downpour 373
The diving 374
There is such a place 375
Some jewels 376

I so indulged my feet 377
Some places time stands still 378
Sleeping by the ocean 379
Sand in the gears 380
What is time? 381
Clouds on Grace Bay 382
Before breakfast 383
Elegant Egret 384
Dizzy 386
Different 387
So you are coming back? 388
Sighing 389
Expectations 390
Light a candle 391
The moon grows towards fullness 392
Bullet train to heart truth 393
So plant the garden 394
Adam 395
Nothing is rushed 396
No doom 397
Seaweed 398

 The River, Time and Tide 

Doubling back 400
I made a list 402
Paris by boat 406
Sweet freshness 408
The walk 409
Abundance 410
Leadership like symphonies 411
Blue roads 412
Current 415
Aching grief 417
Well of silence 419
Circle of silence 420
Thunderclap 421
Now the wind 422
Spirit guides 424
Our music 425
Fortune cookies 427
Spirit guides II 429
Now that I've learned 432
Tides 434
Children don't know a parent 437
Forgiveness II 439
Tundra swans 441
Nature will teach us 442
Haiti 443

Seeking the light 444
Tiny bird 446
Secret life 447

Little Bits from Jottings

Perfection

Perfection
Fails us,
Breaks down,
Eventually,
Disintegrates.
It's being human
That can save us.

www.judysorumbrown.com
judybrown@aol.com

No seed grows

No seed grows
Except by
Breaking through
Its own
Protective coat.

www.judysorumbrown.com
judybrown@aol.com

It is the small space

It is the small space
In our lives,
The daily corner
To which we need repair,
That can create a
Whole new world.
For us,
Vast,
Unconstrained,
And opening.

www.judysorumbrown.com
judybrown@aol.com

Because you have no money

Because you have no money
Don't believe
That you must squander
What you have
In such abundance:
Time together,
Joy,
Attention,
Challenge,
Your good work.

www.judysorumbrown.com
judybrown@aol.com

Everybody Counts

Everybody counts.
When the spider
Weaves the web
No connecting point
Is missed.
If you are missing
From our midst
We are the lesser
For that loss,
And incomplete.

www.judysorumbrown.com
judybrown@aol.com

To sit simply

To sit
Simply
For one sweet hour
And notice
All that is
Unfolding
In the
Light of day—
That is
A fine, fine
Thing.

www.judysorumbrown.com
judybrown@aol.com

Each day dawns

Each day dawns
With its own
Discoveries and surprises,
With its gifts.
If we are home
To all of that
We can't be lost.

www.judysorumbrown.com
judybrown@aol.com

A reservoir within

Each of us needs
A reservoir within,
Because life doesn't happen
On an average.
It has its hurricanes
And droughts,
And lovely days.
So also joy.
So also deep despair.

www.judysorumbrown.com
judybrown@aol.com

I wonder

I wonder
What this day
Will bring
In its unfolding.
Now it begins,
For me,
Like the
Unwrapping
Of an
Unexpected
Gift.

www.judysorumbrown.com
judybrown@aol.com

The Beauty of the Broken

The beauty
Of the broken
And irregular
Is clear
With seashells—
Why not so
With one another?

www.judysorumbrown.com
judybrown@aol.com

Difficult

If it is difficult
Try something
Different.
A tiny shift
Might find
The easy
Natural path,
The one
That's meant
To be.
Persistence
And insistence
May be
Good things —
But not always.

www.judysorumbrown.com
judybrown@aol.com

Spring

Spring
Creeps northward
On her
Annual pilgrimage
Home,
Slowly
Opening blooms
And teaching
Birds to sing.

www.judysorumbrown.com
judybrown@aol.com

Promise

I heard
A bird
Sing
Before dawn—
The gentle
Promise
Of a spring
That's soon
To come.

www.judysorumbrown.com
judybrown@aol.com

Miracle

That the white flower
Has managed
To find light and life,
Making its way
Between the heavy
Patio stones,
Seems such
A miracle
To me,
And even more,
It blooms there,
Planted in such
Seeming solid stone.
It blooms.

www.judysorumbrown.com
judybrown@aol.com

Courage

Certain of the vines
Reach out,
Sending their tendrils
Out and out,
Toward the air,
The sky,
Away from
Anything to
Cling to.
Such vegetative
Courage.

www.judysorumbrown.com
judybrown@aol.com

Mystery

A poem
Should
End
Early,
With the
Mystery
Still intact,
A question
Yet
Unanswered.

www.judysorumbrown.com
judybrown@aol.com

Downpour

The rain
Abates a bit,
Like a mourner
Taking a
Momentary breath,
And then
The downpour
Begins again,
Like a
Great wail
Of water.

www.judysorumbrown.com
judybrown@aol.com

Seasons

There are seasons
Where you
Take in
What you must--
And only later
When the season
Comes
For clearing,
And every Friday
Seven bins of trash
Are sitting at the curb,
(Hauled out as with a
gardener's joy
that finally the thatch
is cleared away),
Only on such a morning
Can we admit
The weight
Of always having taken in
All that we must.

www.judysorumbrown.com
judybrown@aol.com

Surprise

Inevitable,
Yet unpredictable—
So much of life
Is thus:
A hurricane,
The summer's
Heat lightening,
Mortality
And joy.
All take us
By surprise—
Itself surprising.

www.judysorumbrown.com
judybrown@aol.com

Logs

At the heart
Of the fire
Is one
Of the last logs
From the old apple tree
I climbed
Fifty years ago.
Last year it
Simply fell down.
Old, dry
Irregular,
Half-hollowed out,
It burns
Hot
And with ease.

www.judysorumbrown.com
judybrown@aol.com

Tapestry

The memories
Of joys
Sustain us
Through the
Precipice of sorrow
And despair.
It is knowing
The tapestry of life
Is whole
That is life's
Secret.

www.judysorumbrown.com
judybrown@aol.com

Winter

Cold grey
December day
Stares back
At me,
Unblinking.
Sometimes
Winter never
Seems to
Close its eyes.

www.judysorumbrown.com
judybrown@aol.com

Lean Years

Those years—
Those lean years—
Brought the lessons
And awarenesses
I had to have
To find my way
Back home.

www.judysorumbrown.com
judybrown@aol.com

Autumn

Another
Glowing day
Appears.
Another
Autumn glory
Dawns
And spreads its joy
Across the heart.
Those men
Who sing
The praise
Of spring
Have not lived long enough
To know this fall.

www.judysorumbrown.com
judybrown@aol.com

Transition

This is a day
Of transition
To be savoured,
A bridge
Between what is
Now past,
And that to come,
Unknown.
Luminous,
The day rises
To meet us.

www.judysorumbrown.com
judybrown@aol.com

Leaf

Floating
As it was,
Zig-zag and yellow,
I couldn’t tell
If it was
A butterfly
Newly born
Or a leaf
Newly dying.

Grieving

We are softened
By our grievings—
Avoidable and unavoidable
Losses that appear to us
Like apparitions—
Speaking to us
In a language
That we recognize
As if it were
Our native tongue.
However many years
We have,
We have.
Then life
Begins
Another
Round,
A round,
The voices
Ours,
Or others,
Never mind,
The song
Goes on.

Turning Point

She had spent
Most of life
Anxious and agonizing—
Unnecessarily,
As it turned out.
She even sensed
It at the time—
The senseless
Waste of all
That energy.
So she decided
She would stop.
And did.
That was
The turning point.

www.judysorumbrown.com
judybrown@aol.com

Maturity

With maturity
Comes the understanding
That what
Cannot be changed
Must be endured,
Or transformed
Into a mysterious
Adventure.

www.judysorumbrown.com
judybrown@aol.com

Waves

The purple froth
Of the wave edge
Is traced
Upon the salmon sand
At sunset,
And then recedes
To slide gently
Beneath
The next wave
That arrives
To leave
Its whispered mark
Upon the
Ever darkening sand.

www.judysorumbrown.com
judybrown@aol.com

Pelican

The great grey
Pelican
Heads home
At dusk,
Floating
Without an effort
On the currents
Overhead,
Turning a bit
To catch
One wave of air,
Adjusting,
Sailing,
Flying fast
Without a single
Move of wings,
Just floating
Home.

www.judysorumbrown.com
judybrown@aol.com

Magic

The sun
Which frosted
Everything—
The air,
The sky,
The clouds—
A soft sweet pink,
Has disappeared
Behind the clouds.
But for a moment
Magic had descended
With the dawn.
I stood out
On the lawn
And breathed
The pink air in
As if I were
A child,
Enchanted.

www.judysorumbrown.com
judybrown@aol.com

Heart

If I listened
To my heart
I'd know
That it's
Been beating
Just like this
And all along.

www.judysorumbrown.com
judybrown@aol.com

Human

This is
A human
Business,
Being human.
What's
To be
Done?

www.judysorumbrown.com
judybrown@aol.com

Spirit

The native woman
Spoke with tears of anguish
How the Westerners
Think you can own a place:
"How can you own
Something with spirit?"
She had asked us,
Brokenly. Then later
She had said "The spirit
Of a place hold us,
We don't own it."

www.judysorumbrown.com
judybrown@aol.com

Simple Gifts

Sweet gifts

Before she died
she always sent
us luscious ripe
expensive pears
at Christmas time.

This year
completely
unexpectedly
new friends
sent pears
that they
had ordered
from the
very catalog
that she
shopped from.

The pears
arrived
just as hers
would have
for the holidays.

www.judysorumbrown.com
judybrown@aol.com

At Christmas time
my mother always
made her classic
yeasty sweet rolls,
filled with
homemade
candied fruit,
and nuts,
and drizzled
with white icing.

After she died years ago,
I did without,
not even noticing
the loss.

This year
I woke up
from a nap
and rubbing sleep
out of my eyes
I found you
standing
in the hallway,

www.judysorumbrown.com
judybrown@aol.com

Christmas
yeast rolls
in your hand,
"Delivered
one day late,"
you said.

We finish circles
for each other,
stepping into stories
we don't know about,
renewing patterns
for ourselves and
sometimes for each other,
not even knowing
that we do it,
bringing simple gifts,
not guessing how
in doing so,
we draw a circle,
bringing back to life,
our own,
each others too,
sweet complicated things
with deep rich history,

www.judysorumbrown.com
judybrown@aol.com

long lost or just forgotten,
now recalled with puzzled smile,
accepted by our grateful hands,
our lives connected
by each other's
unexpected and sweet gifts.

www.judysorumbrown.com
judybrown@aol.com

Wolf Song

Sometimes when I'm walking
I can hear beside me,
To the left,
The breathing
Of the wolf.

Not like the loons
Out on the pond
Or nearby seagulls,
But an animal
In soul space
Well beyond this place
Within and deep.

There are no footfalls
Of the beast,
No snarls,
Just breathing,
Steady, regular
Like silent journeyer
Conserving energy for
Crossing continents with me.
In silence we walk on.

www.judysorumbrown.com
judybrown@aol.com

They mate for life,
The wolves do.
Does this mean then that
He's my mate,
This wolf beside me,
To my left,
Heeled like some
Well-trained self,
Out of my sight
But with me
Nonetheless,
And breathing evenly?

www.judysorumbrown.com
judybrown@aol.com

Voyager

It is not real, someone might say.
This path is easy. It's not real.
I move as if connected deep within
To some rich source,
My own and not my own,
Drawn forth by words, a touch, a glance,
As if a lightning-bolt has touched my life
Yet softly, without shattering a thing,
Just leaving light and softness,
Mine to touch whenever I am moved to do so,
Or when I am reminded it is there.

I've never known a time like this,
And yet it's quite familiar,
Like coming home to self and to the world,
Like welcoming a voyager
Long gone from these familiar shores
Who now sails back
And seeing the familiar shape of landscape,
Stands in silence

www.judysorumbrown.com
judybrown@aol.com

Drinking in geometry
Of hills and inlets
Known and yet forgotten
In the challenge of the voyage.

I stand upon the gently rolling deck
And simply soak it in,
The landscape of my homeland, heartland,
Knowing in this place from which I've come
I place my feet again,
I plant myself
And am a voyager no more.

Wanting

I've managed to avoid
The pain of loss
By never wanting much,
Never needing what
I still could lose,
Never letting yearning
Of the deepest kind
Rise to the surface
Of my heart and mind.

Now I'm learning
Wanting in a different key,
A different way.

As if I were a tiny child,
I'm learning what it is to
Want with an intensity
That won't let go.

I am alive,
Demanding,
Wanting everything
I can
And cannot have.

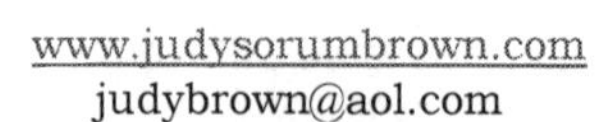
www.judysorumbrown.com
judybrown@aol.com

Before in life,
I've practiced saying "no" to that
Part of myself
That wants, insists.

This time
I practice
Saying "yes."

www.judysorumbrown.com
judybrown@aol.com

Knots

We sat together,
women half a century old,
friends since the day we met
when we were five,
beginning kindergarten.

We traced the paths,
that to a stranger might
seem worlds apart
as well they were,
the scrambled threads
of motorcycle gangs
and drugs and Ph.Ds,
children and broken loves,
tangles with our mortality,
and paths
that brought us
both back home.
Together.
Worlds apart.
To laughter, tears,
and sentences
that trailed off
into a necessary silence.

www.judysorumbrown.com
judybrown@aol.com

"I'd not remembered,"
she said to me, after a pause,
"The way the lake breathes
in the winter when it's frozen solid.
I walked down to the beach
today and I could hear
it breathe again,
as if I were a child."

"And probably you'd never know
that every time I thread a needle
and then knot the end of thread,
I see your mom as she sat here
by this same window, looking
at the lake, and teaching us to sew."

An aging pianist
returns to Moscow
after fifty years.
And we, two, to a
tiny town in Michigan.

We all come home again,
in our own time,
in our own way,
and meet old friends

www.judysorumbrown.com
judybrown@aol.com

whose lives are knotted,
tied to our own tangled threads of living
in a hundred yet unspoken ways,
which we are finding
only now the words to speak.

www.judysorumbrown.com
judybrown@aol.com

Proud

Maybe
he just needs
to know
you're proud of him.

That's not so much
to ask, but dads
don't know they need
to know it,
and besides
they don't know
how to ask.

And maybe he just
needs to hear your voice
and feel your steadiness
as oft I do.

Maybe his calling
is his way of saying,
without words,
he needs
the link with you

www.judysorumbrown.com
judybrown@aol.com

as much as you
once needed him
when he was gone.

And maybe hours
you spent together
recently surprised him
with a hunger
that he didn't know
he had,
and so connection
on the phone
and through the work
are just his way to hold
onto that thread.

And maybe
in the tender rebel,
cautious cynic,
hidden lover
that you are,
he sees himself,
sees choices
that he was afraid
to make,
and calls
to give
encouragement

www.judysorumbrown.com
judybrown@aol.com

or to receive
a blessing
from the man
he thinks of
as his son,
but knows
is mentor
to his dreams
in ways
he cannot speak
and you can never
know, except
when you can hear
the melodies that lie
in silence underneath
the words that sit
so clumsily
in spaces that
emerge in visits
or on phone calls,
never quite connected
and yet linked
at some deep level,
way beyond the words,
forever more.

www.judysorumbrown.com
judybrown@aol.com

Carnations

One day when all
was harsh and hurting,
nothing fit,
and everything I needed
wasn't anywhere around,
he brought carnations
to surprise us all,
red ones, an armful of them,
pink ones too,
but it's the red ones
that I still have now,
weeks later, three of them
tucked in with newer blooms,
as if to not forget
that when our pain
is that the world
around us is ungenerous,
we can always
bring each other flowers.

www.judysorumbrown.com
judybrown@aol.com

Yesterday I bought
some pink carnations at
the grocery store,
smaller and fresher,
not as lavish as his gift.

And as I pushed the grocery cart
toward the store,
intent on getting milk
and coffee and the flowers,
I ran into a friend
I'd not seen since the last time,
months ago, that we had met
exactly in this place,
he heading home as I went in.
And he'd had with him then, as now,
bouquets of flowers.

"Special occasion?" I had asked,
back then. "No" he replied.
"I always buy carnations with
the food. It's just the way
I treat myself."

The pleasure in his voice
seemed to suggest he shared
with me some secret.

www.judysorumbrown.com
judybrown@aol.com

And the pleasure rushed
back over me as yesterday
he called my name, another
armful of the blooms laid in
his cart, reminding me of
men who buy us flowers
as surprises,
and buy flowers for themselves,
and in the joy
of both those acts,
bring beauty back to life
and sweet rememberings
of how we touch
each other
and revive the lives
that are our own,
each others too,
with blossoms,
flowers,
red carnations,
gifts of the spirit,
of the joy of life.

www.judysorumbrown.com
judybrown@aol.com

Poetry again

Today the writing comes as poetry again.
When it was not a poem time
my mind gave reasons,
tried to understand,
built theories,
some with the hope the poems would return
and other theories that were bleak
that feared the voice was gone forever.

The poems probably were somewhere
in the universe, and laughing down at me,
watching my struggle to pretend
my mind could get itself
around a process so beyond my mind.

The poems are already finished,
like a hymn my spirit wrote in 1642
and now my voice sings for the first time
seen by eyes that think it new.
The poem rests within my center self,
a song of heart and soul,
but not of conscious mind at all.

www.judysorumbrown.com
judybrown@aol.com

Rather the poem is the gift
of my whole self
where mind is caught up
in a graceful dance
with other parts of self,
the parts that sweep it off its feet
and swing it round and round
til it is dizzy and entranced
and has forgotten how
to stand so straight
for just a moment.
And wants still more and more
of just that dance
that makes it sing
in ways it didn't know
it could.

www.judysorumbrown.com
judybrown@aol.com

Beyond

Out on the other side of every" no"
there stands a "yes," an affirmation
of the truth.
Beyond each boundary
that we must set
there is on opening
into the infinite.
Each time we face a wall
there is a way unseen
if only turning back
to come again
another day.
Beyond each night
comes dawn;
beyond each dying
is a resurrection morn.

www.judysorumbrown.com
judybrown@aol.com

Grace

She wakens to my
gift to her
for Valentines,
a little furry swan
to snuggle with,
a symbol of how
mothers see a child
who's growing up.
Elated, joyful, then
unaccountably
despairing
that the gift,
so perfect,
yet now opened,
is no more a gift,
she sobs upon
her bed.

Perhaps I too
have lived that way,
grieving because the gift,
exactly what I love,
comes unexpectedly,
or that the package lying opened

www.judysorumbrown.com
judybrown@aol.com

is no longer a surprise.
In the receiving of a gift
I am o'ercome by loss.

Whoever made the little swan
has given her a name:
her tag says "Grace."
And what but "grace"
gives us the wisdom to receive
the gifts of life
when they appear
without the grieving
that they came too soon
or came too late?

Presence

Presence takes energy.
It is a radiance like light,
a holding of oneself,
right here, right now,
as if one were a laser,
light and clear.

I think we're born
with radiance, but lose it
in the growing up,
in thinking that
we must know others more
than we need know ourselves.

Presence is learning
to return to now,
which is of course,
the only place that life can be,
and learning to return to me,
which is of course,
the only instrument
by which I live.

www.judysorumbrown.com
judybrown@aol.com

It is a journey
from the past and future,
both at once,
and from the other
who's out there,
back to the seed of self,
to me, who's here.
It is a coming home.

www.judysorumbrown.com
judybrown@aol.com

Christmas

She wanted pearls,
Long strings of pearls,
Draped on the tree.
But I dismissed
Her plan,
Said there were not
Enough of them
For generosity.

This was my
Perfect tree
Just as it was
Without the pearls.
I didn't listen
To her heart.
I didn't have the
Generosity of spirit
That could hear
Her wisdom for my life:
A tree for two
Is quite a different tree,

A family tree
Has difference
That's woven
In its limbs.

This morning
I got up
And in the dark
I looped long strands
Of pearls
Most carefully
Upon my perfect tree.

It was more
Beautiful by far
Than it had any
Right to be,
More beautiful
Because her presence
And her clarity
(and also pearls)
Had made it so.

www.judysorumbrown.com
judybrown@aol.com

Snow song

I hear spring birds
outside,
singing in snow,
a lilting song,
a celebration of
the unexpected.
How shall I learn
to sing a song of
welcome
for the
unexpected
in my life?

www.judysorumbrown.com
judybrown@aol.com

Dusting of snow

Just a dusting
of snow
on the ground,
enough so urban children
can sleep in
on a school day,
and grown-ups
will think twice
about driving
too fast.
Grace
takes many
forms.

www.judysorumbrown.com
judybrown@aol.com

I cannot know

I cannot know
how your path,
seemingly
so much like mine,
is similar,
is different.

Once I looked
for the answer.
Now I look for
the mystery.

www.judysorumbrown.com
judybrown@aol.com

Sitting on the fence

I grew up on the fence
between the field
and the academy,
sitting and listening
to Dad and farmers
talk about their crops,
watching the dogs play,
growling, circling each other,
feeling the summer's heat,
hearing the insects' hum,
absorbing all of that
into my pores,
my soul.

It isn't any wonder then
that I am always
climbing back upon that fence--
the university on one side
and the field stretched out
before me in the sun.
This is my place,
my heritage,
to live my life
upon this threshhold,

www.judysorumbrown.com
judybrown@aol.com

on this boundary
between two worlds,
coming to see
each has a wisdom
of its own,
coming to find
a hidden wholeness,
uncovering an energy
of life within this place
that first presented itself as a fence
and now becomes a bridge.

www.judysorumbrown.com
judybrown@aol.com

The Pelican

The pelican
Tracing a path
Atop the stormy
Waves reminds me
Of how beauty
Rests not in the
Thing itself,
But in how something
So alive
Dances with this one place
That it is meant to be,
How something
In the nature of
That bird
And in the nature
Of the ocean waves,
Makes patterns,
Natural and graceful,
Beautiful, serene,
In midst of storm.

www.judysorumbrown.com
judybrown@aol.com

So is it when,
with you I
Ride waves unseen,
Afloat in updrafts
We create
By being simply
Who we are.

www.judysorumbrown.com
judybrown@aol.com

They brought new life

They brought new life,
the children did.
Even with divorce
and all its loss,
they brought new life.

They picked up cats
and brought home dogs.
They trailed their
laughing friends
throughout the house.
They filled up carpools
with their laughter
and complaints.
They introduced
complexity and chaos
that distracted me
from work and pain.

They gave us generous gifts and
with persistence they
built lives that were alive
and were their own.

www.judysorumbrown.com
judybrown@aol.com

They loved each other
and loved us,
and humored us
and cherished us.

And now, like gardens
that were fallow,
we're abloom with life.
They've carried us
beyond the deserts
to the other side.
They've made, of us,
a family again.

www.judysorumbrown.com
judybrown@aol.com

I write my way

I write my way
Out of a crisis
Of the soul.
I pull my self
Through darkness
On the tensile
Strength of words,
A rope of rescue
And discovery at once,
As if
Within a cave
I crawl upon
My belly
And then slowly,
I emerge
Into the light.

www.judysorumbrown.com
judybrown@aol.com

There is a turning point

There is a turning point in life
Where having broken
Through our pain, denial,
We are free of our own
Limitations and control,
Past all the points of being
Stuck and deadened.
Frozen in our fears,
There we're no longer
Taking charge
Of life; instead we're riding
Waves of change.

It feels like being in
A natural process,
Foreign and unknown.
We have no knowledge
How the story will unfold,
It hasn't yet.
And we've let go,
With not a chance
of grabbing on again.

www.judysorumbrown.com
judybrown@aol.com

We've given up,
On some old story
That has held us back,
A story which has saved us,
Threatened us, at once.

Past that point
Comes a different
Form of life,
Hard to describe to someone
Who's not traveled there before.
Words fail even for the poet.
There, free and alone, alive,
Not knowing how the
Story ends,
We live within
The hands of God,
If such a God, there be.

www.judysorumbrown.com
judybrown@aol.com

Jungle birds

From Nantucket,
Montreal,
The Outer Banks,
Orlando,
California—
They come flying back now
From summer migrations
With family,
To form the familiar flock
Of girl friends starting school
Together.

Laughing,
Tumbling over each other's stories,
Five voices at once
In ten conversations,
Like beautiful noisy jungle birds
They swoop and fly,
Home once again
Within the canopy
Of their lives.

www.judysorumbrown.com
judybrown@aol.com

The weight of work undone

The weight
Of work undone,
Started too late
To finish well,
Forgotten till the end,
Then patched together
Just in time, slap-dash,
The pain of gifts
Used without grace
Because there wasn't time enough
To let things grow
To their full selves--
Those losses weigh on me
Like little deaths.

A sacred act
Done in a rush
Because there was
No time to do it
From a spirit place,
The things completed
With too little time—

All these spend down my spirit,
Burden me,
Chew at the muscle
Of my heart.

So here and now
I make a vow:
As I would never garden
Without seeds
And rain,
So I will not again
Work without time.

www.judysorumbrown.com
judybrown@aol.com

Winter kite

January not withstanding,
We launched the multicolored
Diamond kite along Lake Michigan,
Into the damp and bitter
Winter wind.

Just as the flurries started,
Spawning flakes like cotton-puffs,
The kite climbed high above the
Snowy beach, and Charley
In his snowsuit, string in hand,
Ran after it,
In hot pursuit,
Until it dove
Into the sand.

There were two swans,
Floating way out,
Serene and white
Upon the gray-green sea.

www.judysorumbrown.com
judybrown@aol.com

It was a momentary miracle,

The swans, the snow, the kite,
And family,
Lasting not long at all,
But long enough,
To lodge itself within
The center of my heart.

www.judysorumbrown.com
judybrown@aol.com

Here I am

Here I am,
Again,
Upon this
Wild ride of a life,
Meeting the words
That pour
Out of my soul,
As one would
Open up
The front door
Of ones home
To some great crowd
Of strangers
And dear friends
Assembled,
And a-chatter,
Bearing casseroles
And gifts,
Come for some matter
Yet known,

For some great celebration
That my soul has
Issued invitations to,
Without the knowledge
Of my conscious self,

Who standing now
Before the door,
Surprised at all
The boisterous noise,
Is glad for the
Surprise.

www.judysorumbrown.com
judybrown@aol.com

My soul votes no

My soul votes no
In odd ways
That I can't control—
By losing things,
By being drawn
To some emerging
Strand of life,
Now newly found
Or rediscovered.

By stubbornly leaning
Up against a door that's closed
And pointing to a universe
That's opening
Another way.

My soul votes no,
And then announces
What it's done,
Whether I like the fact
Or not.

www.judysorumbrown.com
judybrown@aol.com

It doesn't care a whit;
It only wants
One thing for me,
And that
Is life.

www.judysorumbrown.com
judybrown@aol.com

Falling apart

On days
when I'm afraid
that things
will fall apart,
sometimes I learn
to my surprise,
they fall together.

www.judysorumbrown.com
judybrown@aol.com

Grandma Moses talking with Edward R. Murrow

"How do you paint?" he asked her.
She was 95 years old,
Painting trees onto a nearly finished
New England landscape,
Her standard medium--masonite,
Covered with two coats of white paint.

"I paint down" she said.
"I start with the sky,
and then do trees,
and then the ground.
I paint down."
He looked like he expected
Something more complicated
In response.

"And why, Grandma Moses,
have you never painted
anything from the Bible?"
She continued painting the trees.

www.judysorumbrown.com
judybrown@aol.com

"There's a lot unknown
about the Bible. You don't
paint what you don't know."
She went back to painting trees.

The last painting that she did,
When she had passed her century mark,
Was a familiar country scene,
This one, alone among the many,
Had a rainbow.

My friend and I stood looking at it
For the longest time. Held somehow by the
Knowing that it was her last. My friend said
"Look, how the top band of the rainbow,
seems to pull free and rises through the sky,
Beyond the frame and out of sight".

You only paint what you know.

The barns have all burned

The barns
Have all burned,
My friend.

The only hay
Is in the fields,
Sweet and unmowed,

There is good news:
After the raging fires
And loss, we now stand
Knee deep in the luxury
Of open space,
Natural abundance,
Freedom,
Stars all around us.

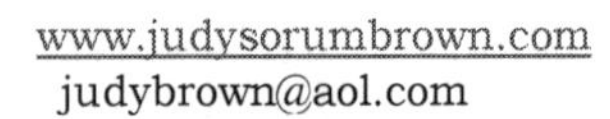
www.judysorumbrown.com
judybrown@aol.com

I turn my head
Into the breezes
At the dawn,
Aware that
This is home
As it is meant to be,
And I am now awake
And in this moment,
Fully, completely
Gratefully alive.

www.judysorumbrown.com
judybrown@aol.com

Two days from solstice

Two days from solstice
In the far Northwest,
The light blooms early,
Tossing the day
Up in the air
Before the world's
Awake
To play
With it.

For Dickens:
We thought we picked you out

We thought we picked you out—
The biggest in the litter,
Just eight days old,
I held you, tiny, in the fold
Of my big sweeping skirt.
You peed on me.
When we returned
To take you home with us,
You'd grown into a
Rotund, golden fluff ball of
Good will and body wagging.
Startled, tiny Meg said, "Are you sure
That he's the one? He is so big."
You were unquestionably ours.
And for a space of seven years
We nursed each other
Through, all of us, sometimes
On little else than spirit
And determination.
You held the center,

www.judysorumbrown.com
judybrown@aol.com

Tail thumping like a metronome
Against the floor
Or wall or chair,
Lying asleep there
In the sunlight,
All aglow, and snoring.
Chasing dreamy rabbits.

Now you are on your way
To somewhere else,
A spirit on the move,
While we are mourning you
It does occur to me:
While we believed
we'd chosen you,
It is more likely
You had chosen us.

www.judysorumbrown.com
judybrown@aol.com

Surrender

It is a moment
Of surrender,
To the sea
That buoys
The kayak,
To the wind
That fills
The sails,
To the day
Unfolding
Freshening
Before us,
To the journey
Now begun,
So much
Unknown,
Lying ahead.

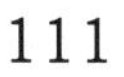

www.judysorumbrown.com
judybrown@aol.com

Urban Libraries

Building
A vast
Monumental library
Sets up
Inevitable resonance
With the homeless,
Left outside
Its polished
And rich spaces,
Now drawn
From the shadows
Into its light.
Meant to be
A space
For the mind,
It ministers
To human bodies—
A bath

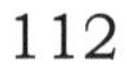

www.judysorumbrown.com
judybrown@aol.com

In the public restroom,
A solace
For the group homes
Never built,
A place away
From the confusion
Of a mind
Losing its place.
The librarians
Are bewildered.
So am I.

www.judysorumbrown.com
judybrown@aol.com

Snow Days

There isn't anything
more full of life and joy
than ones own child
who doesn't have
to go to school
because of snow.

The snowstorms
are an unexpected gift,
a time to snuggle
in a chair before a fire,
a time to play and laugh
and soak the laziness
into our bones,
a time to be
exceedingly undone.

For grown-ups such free days
are rare. Our lives are focused by
the drumbeat of our work,
the cadence of impatient
fingers on a desk

www.judysorumbrown.com
judybrown@aol.com

Perhaps my child's lesson
is one I need to learn:
There isn't anything
more full of
joy and fun,
than one entire day
that's full of snow
and free of everything
I thought was life.

www.judysorumbrown.com
judybrown@aol.com

Wanting II

Crosscurrents
All internal—
The winds of wanting
This which is
The opposite of that
Which I am
Also wanting.
Which is
Essential me?

www.judysorumbrown.com
judybrown@aol.com

Montana

Vast Sky

The sky here is
so vast it can
hold opposites
of weather at
one time—
blue sky, a
storm, a
sunrise,
all at once.

If feelings are
the weather
of the soul,
perhaps
we're all
Montana skies,
quite vast enough
to hold it all.

www.judysorumbrown.com
judybrown@aol.com

Geese

A flock of geese
fly by below me,
in the canyon of the bay,
their calls distinct and clear.
Now suddenly they turn,
and going back
from where they've come,
they round the distant point
are gone.

They never tell you
that the geese can change their mind,
go back, reverse their course.

Those who revere the geese
and speak of how they share the lead,
first one and then the next at point,
they never mention that sometimes the bay,
like this one, into which they've flown,
has walls too high,
or is not what they'd thought,
and so they turn, retracing paths in air,
are gone another way
to somewhere else.

www.judysorumbrown.com
judybrown@aol.com

We owe it to each other
to make sure the story is complete,
of geese and us.

Sometimes the flock is graceful
and determined, knows its way,
and perseveres, arrives.
But other times, the flock reverses and goes back
seeing the way is wrong.
Curious to me, the calls as they swung round
and headed back, seemed not that different
from the calls when I have stood below
vast flocks that headed north and never wavered
from their course.
I wonder what the
leader said just now to help them turn?
I only know the tone seemed just the same,
clear and encouraging,
as when the flock is flying straight
and needn't change its course at all.

www.judysorumbrown.com
judybrown@aol.com

The Storm

Now comes the sun in splendor
in the pines across the ridge,
the peach sky turns to golden-blue,
the ridges from black-blue
to gray and lavender.

When water turned black-green the other day,
I knew the storm would come.
I paddled kayak steadily for shore
before a wall of rain and hail
drove hard across the lake
obliterating sky and mountains cross the way.

I told the others
I could smell the storm
before it came.
It smells quite beautiful,
a storm does,
like a clearness
carrying the smell of spruce along the shore,
as when I pass someone out on the street
and hold just for a moment
that light scent they wear, in wonder.

www.judysorumbrown.com
judybrown@aol.com

So here the wind and rain,
the sentinels of pine,
sweet messages mixed with
the shocks of lightening,
a danger real and mortal,
all wrapped within a moment
in a kayak:
beauty, danger, challenge,
harsh reality and luck,
the strength to paddle,
and the providence
to smell the storm in time.

www.judysorumbrown.com
judybrown@aol.com

Flash floods

At ten to seven, sun is up.
How does a sunrise
lead to memories of a storm?
The mind has
strange connections
at its heart.
It links and weaves
in ways we can't
anticipate,
running down
streams we didn't
know about,
the way a flash flood
in the mountains
changes rocky stream-bed
to a raging river
without warning.
So do storms of heart and soul
produce flash floods
that race through us
and then are gone.

www.judysorumbrown.com
judybrown@aol.com

Waves on Deep Bay

It doesn't look like
there are waves upon
the lake, but I can
hear them hit the shore
way, way below—the
steady breathing of one wave,
a silence, then the next.

Sometimes my world,
my life, seem calm just
like this lake, the waves
not visible but heard
against a distant shore,
a whispered message
sighing in the steady
pattern of a wave
and then the silence
of a trough.

I wonder if our voices
speaking words of justice and humanity,
of love and welcome,
voices that we sometimes feel are lost,
are never really lost at all,
but heard within a larger pattern over time,
the message not, as we have come to think,

www.judysorumbrown.com
judybrown@aol.com

within a single wave,
but rather in the patterns over time,
a trough of silence followed by
the whisper of another wave,
best heard when listened for near dawn,
as I am listening now,
this grey and misty cool
Montana morning,
high up above Deep Bay
as waves speak messages,
first one and then the next,
against the shore below.

www.judysorumbrown.com
judybrown@aol.com

Seeing complexity

You'd think it had
a simple symmetry
this maple leaf.
We think we know
about a leaf.
But this one is
some complicated
road map of a
country unfamiliar
and unique,
aberrant, disorganized,
chaotic, in a way
I hadn't wanted to
admit about a leaf.
Or of myself.
Or of this place.
Or you.
I'd wanted
to believe
a simpler truth
about it all.

www.judysorumbrown.com
judybrown@aol.com

And of the leaf,
I hoped to say
I understood it,
saw it as it was,
right from the start.
But as I spent more time
with it, like you and me,
and life and work,
both yours and mine,
it held daunting complexity,
surprises and stark simplicity
All at one time.

www.judysorumbrown.com
judybrown@aol.com

Dawn storm

A storm is visible
off to the right,
grey, dark,
a lightning strike
appears;
and on the left,
a peach dawn
opens glorious.

The two are
side by side.
So life.

The storm
beside the dawning light,
within a single moment,
both are there.

The fear and terror live
right here beside the love.

Still, as I watch,
the lightning flashes,
and the breeze at dawn
is fresh and clear,
not because dawn

alone refreshes,
but because the storm
has washed the air,
refreshing me as well.

Webs

Now dawning
sunlight
touches
spider webs,
the sheerest kind
stretched in between
the plants,
across the lawn.

The webs of
feeling.
meaning,
touch,
between us,
are that fine.

www.judysorumbrown.com
judybrown@aol.com

Hummingbirds asleep

When do the humming birds
Get naps? When do they sleep?
The tiny helicopter-birds,
Buzzing about their busy business
All day long are nowhere to be found
At four fifteen
With dawn an hour away.

When they're at rest, they're gone.
Evaporated. They don't exist.
It's only busyness, activity
Gives them their visibility,
Their realness in our eyes.

Maybe we think the same of us.
Without our work,
Activity,
We disappear,
Or so we fear.

www.judysorumbrown.com
judybrown@aol.com

A sense of place

A sense of place
is just a sense of
spirit, not an owning

A sense of place
is some fine sense
of sacredness
beyond the words
of even poetry

It's in the slant of light
upon the field,
the stars against the inky sky,
a silence welcoming,
the mountain and the wood..

A sense of place
comes from a heritage
of deep respect,
and from being with a place
for just however long
we're given to be there.

www.judysorumbrown.com
judybrown@aol.com

Courage

Bells

Each time the link's electric,
stunning, I awake and know
the voice is speaking in me of
the possible, the thing I know is true.

Be still small voice within and
give me time and space to think or
thinking not I will say "yes"
because my heart speaks openly.

An open heart is fearsome, silent,
sad and joyful all at once, a
great bell tolling news of peace
and war and famine and of love.

How shall I silence it once it
is known to me? The ringing
true of bells within once heard
across the square, the secret's out.

And you will know and
understand the news and
bow your head and feel my
tears as if they were your own.

www.judysorumbrown.com
judybrown@aol.com

Courage II

I was on my way
to meet with you,
when suddenly I noticed that
the car ahead of me had
"courage" spelled out on its
license plate, an unexpected
message in a universe of work.

A little red car, with some
woman at the wheel,
with "courage" as her message
to me. Staying just ahead of
me, she led me for a while,
taking the same route
that I always take,
and then turned left into
a monastery.
And my mind
went on to what
we'd talk about at work,
and I forgot
her message for a while.
Who was her message for?
Herself? Or you? Or me? All three?

www.judysorumbrown.com
judybrown@aol.com

What does it mean to be courageous
following some stranger whose red car
bears such a word? Does it mean that
as we work we live? By courage?
Should we then speak our truth?
Or listen? Perserve?
Give up? How do we know?

Courage is a moving thing,
like little red cars
that we follow,
driven by some stranger
who turns left before us
and is gone,
leaving us alone
and in the silence of our soul
to find the courage that is ours
alone.

www.judysorumbrown.com
judybrown@aol.com

Lace Candlelight

Lace candlelight upon my page,
before the dawn you draw the
pen across the sheet of white
and coax the secrets from
the space long hidden
from myself.

I look with curiosity and wonder
as the blue ink weaves and tugs at
strands I didn't know about--
the candle like a gentle sentinel
sits to the left, so shadows point
the way as words uncoil upon
the page.

By candlelight the shy words
venture out, the little shy ideas,
suggestions of the soul,
the hidden quiet self, the
waiting one, waiting from
cross the centuries and continents
to be offered this soft opening
to the day, to consciousness, to light.

www.judysorumbrown.com
judybrown@aol.com

Moments open

This summer as I walked the roads in Maine
my thoughts came out as poetry
and colors vibrant, sharp
danced in the trees.

One day a stranger walked ahead of me
and when he paused to take a
pebble from his shoe, we spoke
of death and dying and of grief.

A chance exchange but to the
heart of what it means to journey
with a dying spouse and to remember
raw recruits, Marines, dead on a hill
decades ago.

Now other moments open
too whenever strangers meet or
friends connect again, straight
to the core, as if the heart is barely covered,
nor seeks a cover, just
kindred souls and chance connections
as mysterious and unexpected as
the poems.

www.judysorumbrown.com
judybrown@aol.com

Traps

Prestige and title,
rank, security--
are all, perhaps,
for the ambitious,
rusty traps
that lunge at us
or we lunge into,
hungry for our
place in worlds
not seeming safe.

Greeting jagged jaws
as welcoming,
we willingly
put foot in trap,
believing it is solid ground
and later think
as wounds heal,
that we might have chosen
otherwise
but learned much less
in doing so
about the path
that is our own.

www.judysorumbrown.com
judybrown@aol.com

Snow

The snow is waiting there in Michigan,
like I remember from my childhood days,
great banks of snow obscuring cars and shrubs,
snow hard and heavy, leaden,
snow screaming in the blizzard wind,
snow silent, dropping like great
feather loads of cotton, piling on the branches,
mounds of snow to roll in, dive in,
pelt each other with, and laugh.
The snow that skis slide over easily.
The solace of such welcome snow.
Its silence and its peace.

Where I live now, there's not such snow.
Occasionally we get a dusting, but it seldom stays.

There's something lost in living
where the snow has no time of its own,
no season where it reigns,
no month in which it is our master
and we make our lives within its grip,
no time when every day we turn our face
up to the sky and feel its snowy fingertips
caress our cheeks so cooly, gently.
There's knowing there about a side of life
lost to us living in more southern climes,

www.judysorumbrown.com
judybrown@aol.com

a knowing how the rains can take a different form,
material, almost permanent and beautiful at times.
There's understanding in the flakes of snow,
about our lives, our passage on this earth,
our past and future too.

And so when I return to Michigan
and stand with arms outstretched
and catch a snowflake on my tongue
and taste it, laughing, and another too,
it is a reading of reality, of life,
like picking up a novel only partly read
or poem long forgotten and then nodding
as we recognize the story there, and recollect
how true it is for us as well.

www.judysorumbrown.com
judybrown@aol.com

Moved

"I moved too much," she said to me
not long before she died. "I moved
too much. Don't do that. It's not good."

How do we move too much?
By giving up our roots to follow
one we love
who longs for a
geography that's different
from the one etched on our soul?
By giving up the things we're certain of
because the others certainty is more insistent?
By giving up the center
which speaks clearly to our soul
and moving to a different space
where we catch only whispers
of that voice? By setting things aside
that give us joy, to watch the other
sleeping, working, playing?
She spoke as of geography and moving vans,
and yet there was much more behind those words.
I listen to her now in ways I couldn't then.
Her voice is with me like a mantra, whispered:
"Don't move too much; it isn't good."

www.judysorumbrown.com
judybrown@aol.com

Calling

Something is calling me. I try to hide it from myself.
I feel the pull and still I stand my ground.
Why do I turn my face aside and look away?
Why when I'm called do I stand silent,
noticing the strength it takes to bite my tongue,
to hold the answer deep within,
where even I am never sure how clear its voice,
how strong its words?

Something is calling me. I feel it sometimes as a
hunger in myself or in the other. Yearning
maybe. Incompletion. As if I were the
second half of something beautiful from
which I'm lost. From which I've wandered off,
distracted, even happy, at first not knowing
how I separated from whatever once was there.

As if in sometime long ago or deep within
there was a place of home and I've now
lost the map. But I've lived now so long
within this other territory, with this empty space,
that when the calling comes and from that place,
I look for someone else's voice and
not for that which calls to me within,
and from eternity at once.

www.judysorumbrown.com
judybrown@aol.com

It's like a labyrinth, this musing on the call.
I know when I have answered it
in smaller ways, the call to come together
in a learning place, to take the conversation
to a deeper well of questions, solace,
when that small call is answered, there's a grace,
a showering of gifts that if I let myself,
would bring my tears of thanks.

Perhaps that's why I bite my tongue.
I fear the flow of tears. The gratitude.
What would it feel like to answer
and to say what would be said in honesty,
once I stepped in that place? What choices
would array themselves, compelling,
natural, impossible, to which my heart
and spirit would say "yes" at once,
and tell me later what they'd done?
I fear the tears of gratitude and learning
from the heart of me that I am on a path
we've chosen not with knowing parts of me
but with my soul.

Perhaps today it is a call I'll answer.
And maybe not. We'll see.

www.judysorumbrown.com
judybrown@aol.com

Healing

I write in moonlight and in candlelight.
The coffee steams within the mug before me
and as I look up at the blooming plants,
your healing is what touches me.

You've healed my heart,
you who call me healer, priestess,
you have healed and mended me,
have opened me into a self within
that waits here for me.
You have given me the gift of me.

You've slowed me down,
or to be more precise,
you've stopped me in my tracks.

Sometimes I wonder
if you've healed me with your hands
or just your spirit.
The means is unimportant,
but I know the feeling
of one hardened who is
breaking out of something crusted,
out of something like a grave
and into life.

www.judysorumbrown.com
judybrown@aol.com

Have you prayed for me?
For what will be?
They say that that's the prayer
that works the best with seeds,
just "what will be."
And I feel like a seed that's
waited here for centuries,
now touched by some fine rain,
or dewdrops, given ground
in which to grow,
to stretch into the time to come.

www.judysorumbrown.com
judybrown@aol.com

Needed

You came into my life
as if I asked for you,
I begged that you be sent.
Long before knowing
what the questions were
I knew I needed you beside me,
in the inquiry.

You came into my life
like dawn. At first
I didn't notice you at all
as I do now, but in the
corner of my eye, I wondered
at your presence, wondered
and then shook my head a bit
and kept my eyes ahead.

You came into my life
because I needed you to live.
It's just that simple,
nothing more complex.
And so you're here.

www.judysorumbrown.com
judybrown@aol.com

Some days you're standing
here before me.
At other times, you're simply
in my heart working a healing
magic for my soul,
whispering the words of
recollection or imagining that
come as poetry.

They're yours,
they're mine, these words,
I never can tell whose,
now that you're here,
but listen to their hope
and healing that is yours,
and mine, and all the world's, forever more.

www.judysorumbrown.com
judybrown@aol.com

Invitation

You and I
are each an
invitation
to the other
from a space
within ourselves
we do not know
and yet we will,
as time
unfolds us.

We think
the invitation strange,
as if it comes
from some address
we don't yet recognize.

We look down at it
curious, wondering, confused,
so set it now aside
as if it comes to us
by error.

www.judysorumbrown.com
judybrown@aol.com

Yet when we pick
the invitation up again
we sense it is
indeed for us,
but we can't
fathom why it's come.
or what it's for.
or what it asks
that we now do.
And so we stand
feeling a little strange,
a little fearful,
giddy even, light-headed,
We run our fingers
down the edges
of the envelope unopened,
hesitant to find what is within,
since with increasing
certainty beyond deciding
we know the answer is
a wordless "yes."

www.judysorumbrown.com
judybrown@aol.com

Courage II

"Courage starts with caring"
I think Pooh told Piglet, once.
But where does courage end?
Perhaps it never ends.

Perhaps it's present
every moment that we opt
for truth, each time
we let ourselves be broken open.
Perhaps it stands in
deep appreciation when
we enter dialogue and
know we will be changed.
Perhaps it puts an arm
around our shoulders
every time we step into the pain
of life's impossible and necessary
paradoxes and stand firm
though shaken to the core.
Perhaps it's a warm hand
in friendship
extended from a generous heart
when we reach
well beyond capacity.

www.judysorumbrown.com
judybrown@aol.com

And maybe we will never
get it right, but simply
hope that caring deeply as we must,
the courage will appear
when necessary.

www.judysorumbrown.com
judybrown@aol.com

Arms

I gave you all the
ammunition that you needed
to keep me at arms length forever.
My panicked fear at wanting you
was so intense I gave you
every weapon I could find
to help you stand on guard
against my heart.

I armed you with the honest
tales of my bad choices in the past;
I armed you with my boundaries
so I could tell myself each time
the yearning in me rose,
the boundaries were yours, not mine,
and if I stepped across the DMZ
I'd lose the friendship that I prize.
And so I haven't moved an inch.

I told you stories that you'd
take as signal you were one of
many in my life, so that neither you nor I would
understand the stunning truth that I'd
unearthed--that I now needed you as I have
never needed anyone before.

www.judysorumbrown.com
judybrown@aol.com

You added all my armaments to your own set,
built of your caring and your fearing and your scars.
I knew I wasn't strong enough
to keep the rules of war straight on my own.
I was so scared of loving you I thought I'd die.
And so I staged a fine pre-emptive strike
for you to lead, but I survived.

And when I did all this those many
months ago, I knew I did it for the
best of reasons: it was what
responsibility to you and to myself required.

But while my mind was arming
you and me with logic and with rules,
and while my fears were telling me in
graphic terms the costs of caring for you,
in the chasm of uncertainty that yawned before me,
while all my fears of having you, not having you and
losing you,
welled up with waves of tears, way, way beyond
my strength to fight them back,
yet all that time,
these poems quietly were spinning out their words,
unlocking every entrance as I sealed it off,
climbing the very walls I'd built between us,
telling us a deeper truth.

www.judysorumbrown.com
judybrown@aol.com

I lay down arms.
I've lost the war.
This is a clear surrender.
I've failed in every graceless
effort to lock up the very doors
you've helped me open to myself.

And so I'm standing here in terror
at discovering
that what I've wanted for so long within my life,
has found its way into my heart,
despite my best defense,
and I have lacked the courage
to admit it to myself,
much less to you.

www.judysorumbrown.com
judybrown@aol.com

Feelings

How can the pain of feelings long ignored
slam into me with such a vicious force,
like animals that tear at some soft gut
of prey who glancing elsewhere is
distracted at the moment of attack?

How can the pain sit heavily on me,
a leaden force of weight
that strains my thigh muscles
and drags my center down into itself
where it remembers in a body's way
the pain unnoticed at the time,
as if the hurt is all stacked up
like little burdens, deep within,
until the camel falls upon its knees.

I'd hardened to my pain these many years,
the little scrapes, abrasions of a life.
They never seemed worth mentioning
right then. There wasn't time.
Besides I knew you didn't like the sight of blood.
I'd wipe the telltale drops from consciousness and
get right on about the business of our life.

www.judysorumbrown.com
judybrown@aol.com

I didn't realize then that the blood was
from the stitches we were tearing out
that held the person I was whole,
that let me be who I am deep within.
I didn't know.

Now that the wrenching hurt can
be ignored no longer,
I float, am helpless in the waves
of pain and sadness that pour over me.

www.judysorumbrown.com
judybrown@aol.com

Chair

I left a chair for you
as we drew close within
the circle. Within my
mind's eye you were with
us in the work, and in the
quiet contemplation
of how love emerges
among strangers,
gently, shyly,
like fine, fine mist of early rain
that settles on our upturned faces,
and over time becomes a downpour till we say
with some surprise,
"that snuck up on me,
all the rain did,
and the power of the storm..."

Perhaps the earth
is shy of rain,
as we are shy of love,
yet parched,
as if in drinking deeply,
we first notice with surprise
that we've been thirsty.

www.judysorumbrown.com
judybrown@aol.com

I left a chair for you as we drew close,
because it is your gift to be
in quiet inquiry, to wonder
how the world and work could be
if we could be less shy
in listening each other into life and voice,
as if the reaching out to one another
as we now do in unguarded moments
were our natural way.

I left a chair for you
because of others drawing close
who knowing all your gifts
would certainly have drawn
you in without my mentioning your name,
and also as a gift to those whom
you don't know yet, men of
heart and spirit, women too,
who instantly would recognize you as their kin
and hug you home.

But in my heart of hearts,
I held a chair for you because
whenever life takes me to deeper
wells of spirit, feeling, I have
come to know that
you belong within that space.

www.judysorumbrown.com
judybrown@aol.com

The circle isn't quite complete,
my center self not home and settled
till your spirit joins the group.

And so I hold the chair
and welcome you
yet once again.

Cries

The wind chimes ring,
as if this beach house is
a mountain top retreat
in some far, foreign land.
Bach organ music plays on low.
The loons call.

Cathedral sounds,
these are, and from
another place and time.

They say the loons
call out in celebration
when a baby's born,
a little loon.
Perhaps they cry
in sadness, too,
when dreams die.
Or when their nests
are filled with water
and must be left behind
for some new place.

www.judysorumbrown.com
judybrown@aol.com

Perhaps those are their cries
as well. The sad cries.
At dawn, the cries
seem celebrational and hopeful,
but in the deepest night the sounds
float lost, forlorn,
alone and sad
beyond the power of my words
to tell.

www.judysorumbrown.com
judybrown@aol.com

Cathedral

This house is like a tiny
church within a wood,
built for forever: copper roof,
hewn beams, stone chimney,
granite steps.

What does it mean
to build so permanently
in the face of change?
Is it a dance with
nature or a gauntlet?
Is it a gift to all
or shoveling the sea?

By holding to the holdings
are we only chanting incantations,
modern magic to dispel the fears,
uncertainties of being human?

Is it a stewardship of
deep responsibility
or just the fear
of our own immortality
that keeps us building so,
and clearing land,
and plowing, fencing, owning?

www.judysorumbrown.com
judybrown@aol.com

When what we know so deep within
is that the world holds us,
not we the world.

Or that the holdings
hold us in the world
and owning the cathedral
keeps our spirits
tied to the material,
when spirits long to soar,
to step outside of daily duties
dictated by holdings,
flying free instead
to weave a magic
of a different kind,
cathedrals of a different sort,
sweet spirit places
for the soul
now busy building
churches for the world
and tired to the bone
from lifting stones
and hewing beams
that make
this stunning place
reality.

www.judysorumbrown.com
judybrown@aol.com

Alone

You leave me space
to be alone with you.
We sit in silence
and are whole.

When there are words
they touch my heart
and yet the wordless times
are like a tonic to my soul.

I'm curious how this works,
this healing quiet
in a world of chaos,
jangle, noise.

It is a puzzle to me,
welcome, though, this
way we are in friendship,
sometimes speaking,
sometimes silent,
oft in laughter,
sometimes tears.

www.judysorumbrown.com
judybrown@aol.com

We are alone the way
the trees are,
standing solid,
side by side in silence,
face into winds,
listening together to the echoed
silence of a night,
individual and unmoving,
steady to ourselves
and to each other,
like old friends
who needn't speak
to know each other close.

www.judysorumbrown.com
judybrown@aol.com

Dreamed

You dreamed me into being;
I dream you in my life
so I can learn from you, my friend,
all that you've lived,
so I can feel it in my heart
and know the way in which
it's true for me as well.

You dreamed me out of numbness,
out of giving up and giving in.
You pulled me to my feet
and helped me dust the leaves
and grit off of my spirit.
You helped me wake my heart.

You did all this as childhood
playmates do, in natural ways,
as they are busy building forts
or climbing trees or
racing through the fields.
Even if I stumble
I can count on your sure hand
to reach for me, so I can
catch myself before I fall.

www.judysorumbrown.com
judybrown@aol.com

And so I dream of you,
in day dreams and most unexpectedly
in night dreams too, dreams where
I'm traveling or facing some new fear,
then you are there to keep me company
or steady me when things are rough.

My dreaming partner, you've become.
Unnoticed by us both, you've moved
into that spirit place and settled in,
in comfort without words.
I love you there.
I dream you'll stay.

www.judysorumbrown.com
judybrown@aol.com

If you were sick

If you were sick,
What then? What
Would you then do that
You can't do now?
Won't do because the
Price is just too great?
But would do then
Because to not do it
Would risk your soul
When yet too little
Time remains?

If you were sick,
What then? What
Questions would be
Answered quickly,
Easily, about who
Then would care and how,
And when, and at what price
And with what joy?

If you were sick,
What then?
Which choices
Much too hard
To make right now

Would then be made
Quite easily? What
Promises that now
Are yokes would
Be recalled and either
Easily fulfilled or
Set aside?

If you were sick
What dread discomfort
Could be seen with
Clear relief, what pain
Acknowledged and removed
By caring hands, what
Tears of fear and hurt and pain
Could then be shed
Quite openly and then be
Wiped away?
What welcome
And safe harbor could be found
With mooring free?

If you were sick,
What place of comfort,
Care, relief and welcome
Long forgotten could appear
Again within your life
And be accepted and

www.judysorumbrown.com
judybrown@aol.com

Acknowledged,
Take its rightful spot and
Wrap your heart and spirit
In a lasting warmth
That's trustable and welcome
Even though you
Say you like the cold?

If you were sick
What price would you
Then know you'd paid,
Sufficient to redeem your life
As yours alone to live,
In freedom and responsibility,
Welcoming you home within yourself,
And placing arms of comfort round you,
Resting hand on shoulder,
Guide you through the doorway,
Motion you to life, to a vitality
That beckons you from all directions
To the earth and
To eternity at once?

If you were sick
What compromises and excuses,
Solid reasons not to move
Would suddenly evaporate
Before your eyes? Or what

www.judysorumbrown.com
judybrown@aol.com

Deep dreams that matter so
Could you then set aside? Or
Make commitment to? Or
What impossibility you yearn for
Would then seem the natural
Way, inevitable?

If you were sick
What health would then
Be possible? What
New vitality, what
Longed-for life that
You have present in your
World right now would speak for you--
Vitality which you keep well walled-off,
So that it seems the power of disease alone
Can smash you through that barrier to life?
It is a wall that your deep
Healing self could scale
In one light bounding jump,
With joy, with life, and laughing
Walk straight to the field that lies ahead.
If you could answer
Why you hold disease within,
Hold sickness as a key to health,
Your healthy soul
Would answer
With your life.

www.judysorumbrown.com
judybrown@aol.com

Being

The way we are connected
calls for no action,
only being.

It doesn't ask
that we decide,
or choose,
or do,
just that we are.

It doesn't point
to some new life
we should arrange,
but what we have.

Right now.
Together,
and apart.

www.judysorumbrown.com
judybrown@aol.com

Lone seagull

Lone seagull
Dives for breakfast
In the creek—
This time,
The fourth dive,
He can barely
Take off
With his catch.
Sometimes
Success
Brings its own
Challenges.

www.judysorumbrown.com
judybrown@aol.com

Island in the Center Of the Heart

Wilderness within

I hadn't planned to weave
together poems
about nature with
the love songs--
poems of the natural,
with poems of the wilderness
within. I had no
thought to
give them all
to you to read
so you could
read between
the lines
whatever's natural
for you to hear
within these words--
so you could savor,
what bears savoring,
as one would listen
deeply to a bird song
in a wood,
or stand
in dappled light
transfixed.

www.judysorumbrown.com
judybrown@aol.com

It never had occurred
to me to do this as a gift,
a weaving sent with gratitude
for what you've given me,
and for the courage that
I've seen in you--
until this morning I awoke,
and it was all I longed to do.

www.judysorumbrown.com
judybrown@aol.com

Longing II

I felt the longing
long ago
and let it be,
away from me,
unspoken,
unacknowledged,
let it go,
so you and I would know
I could be trusted
to leave space and privacy--
to honor who you were
and where we both
were in our lives.

I thought
that it was
only me who
felt that
chemistry.

Today you
let me feel
that longing
once again,

www.judysorumbrown.com
judybrown@aol.com

and let me
know
you felt
it too.

It was
an act of
courage, grace
and generosity.
I'm still
so stunned, confused
at having felt
the gift
of your
clear honesty
that I am struggling
to write poetry
that touches it
as you've touched me.

www.judysorumbrown.com
judybrown@aol.com

Wind

Nothing is lost forever
if we come to think
in ways yet large enough
to hold it all.

The things that burn or die
are dust still blowing in the wind.
Out on a night like this
they ride the waves,
and so do we,
when we are dying
and still being
born again.

www.judysorumbrown.com
judybrown@aol.com

Seasons II

The seasons turn from one into another
Whether we have noticed
They have come and gone or not;
So are we linked at some deep level
Even when we're unaware of that strong bond.
And just as first snow or an early blossom
Startles and delights us,
So does seeing suddenly the evidence of
Kinship startle and delight.

Yet maybe such a link between our hearts is natural,
To be awaited with anticipation,
As we await return of spring
Or the first snowflake on our face,
And all that keeps us from the knowing
It would come of course in time,
Is simple lack of faith and failing
To discern its presence in our lives
Once it arrives.

The seasons blur into each other,
Taking with a grain of salt
Our firm insistence on their separateness,
Their boundaries.

www.judysorumbrown.com
judybrown@aol.com

Perhaps we blur into each other, too,
Despite insisting on the ways we are apart.
I know that sense of boundaries interweaving
When your soft wondering reveals a question
Deep within my soul
I've never called to voice
Until you spoke it into being.

How is it that
The boundaries and edges of the self
Can reach like searching hands
So naturally to clasp the other close,
As on a single day in April
When the spring and winter
Live within a single moment,
And snow sifts down on daffodils,
Or in the height of August heat
When maple leaves begin to
Tinge with red, and autumn's evident
Within the summer's heart?

So is your heart and spirit in my mind
While I am thinking of my separateness,
And how we differ.
Yet are we kindred parts of one reality,

www.judysorumbrown.com
judybrown@aol.com

A flow of deep connection
So essential and so fundamental
That it carries us along, together
Without our knowing how it's so.

www.judysorumbrown.com
judybrown@aol.com

He asked me

He asked me
if this one,
this woman
whom he'd met,
was "it", the
one he waited for.

I listened
to his struggle
to decide
upon which meeting
he should act.
And then I knew
a truth, for him
as well as me:
each time that
we are drawn to
someone
it's a notice
from our heart
about what touches us,
what draws us out of
loss and fear,

www.judysorumbrown.com
judybrown@aol.com

what bids us
welcome to the world,
again,
what summons
all our tenderness.

And it is also true,
each woman
whom he sees
is news
about who's
drawn to him,
who feels a
fit of sorts
with him,
who finds with him
a gift, a joy.

Yet greater news
is news of him,
of life stirring within.

When in the eyes of each
one whom he passes,
he is looking for that perfect one
whom he can hold and love,

www.judysorumbrown.com
judybrown@aol.com

the one who's "all of it"--
he misses the more powerful news:
this longing's not
so much about
the women whom he
meets and loves,
but rather it's
the story of himself
and his capacity
to care
and to be cared for,
now, and every moment
that he lives.

Perhaps he shouldn't choose.
He need just listen
to the wisdom of his heart
as it feels once again
what it has had capacity
to feel, and reaches out
upon its own, to taste
to touch, to feel
that which the universe
wants him to have.

www.judysorumbrown.com
judybrown@aol.com

Solitude II

In moonlit foggy darkness
before dawn,
silent in kayak,
I trailed three loons north,
up the center of the pond.

The surface of the water
was a mirror
touched by soft
spiderwebs of fog.

They cut a wake,
the loons did,
fanning gentle ripples out behind,
a path that I could see,
and follow easily.

They seemed to know
that I was there,
at thirty paces to their rear,
as if a human being lost,
I needed guidance
on my way.

www.judysorumbrown.com
judybrown@aol.com

From time to time
one of the three
would pause
and turning head,
look back at me,
as if to make sure
I was still behind.

They never dove.
They never wavered
from their course.
They made no sound,
but for an hour or so
they led me north along a path
the moon was tracing
in our wake,
we four,
three loons and me.

They reach
across millennia to us,
the loons do,
linking with a human species
younger to this earth by far than they,
teaching us solitude
and wisdom about journeying,

www.judysorumbrown.com
judybrown@aol.com

drawing a path before us,
if, as on a moonlit August morning,
we can paddle silently
and follow
where they lead.

www.judysorumbrown.com
judybrown@aol.com

Time

The woods in Maine in summertime
remind me how the color green
is not one thing,
but many different shades:
the solid green of fern matured,
the purple green of skunk cabbage,
the soft sage green of moss upon a log long dead,
the yellow green of pine needles
that catch the sun and drench
themselves in gold,
the greens that shade off into black or
brown or moldering chartreuse.

Time is like that.
Not just a simple, single thing.
A moment is not just one thing
but many shades of meaning,
hues of life, shaped, stretched,
elongated, transformed by light
and by a soft vitality which time
like pine branches,
is drenched with, bathed with,
so that the air around such moments
fills with golden dust,

www.judysorumbrown.com
judybrown@aol.com

and like the branches,
once a single simple green,
such moments are alive
with timeless life.

www.judysorumbrown.com
judybrown@aol.com

Ceremonies

Ceremonies are the clay
from which we mold the
meaning of our life,
the water which we
wash the wounds with,
bandages that soothe and
keep the healing clean and safe.
Small ceremonies like the
candle to the side
while I now write,
or just one cup of tea,
or peaceful walks along old paths,
or skipping stones along a beach
we walked in childhood.
New ceremonies like the
birthday marking half a century,
or old hurts written on the slips of paper
burned and ashes thrown into the sea,
or consecrating houses newly built
with laughter and the presence
of our friends and music.

www.judysorumbrown.com
judybrown@aol.com

Ceremony is a way to notice,
just a way to breath it in,
this passage through a special time,
not to forget the depth of life
as it rolls by along the surface of our seeing.
Take it deep within instead in rites
that stop the horizontal march of time
and pull time down into our center,
weave it with our soul,
braid it in golden patterns
richly seen in moonlight,
felt gently, joyfully, deeper still,
til it belongs to all the universe together.
A breath of meaning, life,
a moment felt by all,
a desert ride on horseback
in the silence of the night
without a moon by starlight,
noticing the texture of our being
and the fine, fine silence of our soul.

www.judysorumbrown.com
judybrown@aol.com

Feather

I am a feather
Resting in the wind,
Floating on the tide,
Reminder of a
Bird who passed
This way,
A feather
Free and light,
Light like a dream
Or dust that hangs
Suspended
In a ray of sun
Within a wood,
Light like the call
Of distant song bird,
Almost without
Weight at all,
At one with wind
And tide
And ground.

www.judysorumbrown.com
judybrown@aol.com

I am like fire,
A soft and feathery flame,
Touched by the wind
And moved by it.
I cross the fields
In moments,
By an energy
That is not mine alone,
But is the energy
Of fire
And wind
And ground
That's covered
With dry grass.

I am a feather
Like the flames
That clear
The springtime fields
Of thatch.
I travel with an energy
That is the echo
Of my loving you.

www.judysorumbrown.com
judybrown@aol.com

I float on songs,
Your smile,
Your wonder
And your laugh,
Upon those
Open moments
When the winds
Blow freely
Through the forest
Of your soul.

Upon those currents
I am carried
Without care
And without needing
To be told
Whence winds like that
Will travel me.

I ride them freely, safely,
Tossed sometimes in storms
And sometimes
Floating in an eddy
Of the tide
You are
Within my life.

www.judysorumbrown.com
judybrown@aol.com

Circles

From pebbles in a pond,
from center point and out
the circles move,
further and further,
til they are no longer seen at all,
no longer different from the water's
rippled surface.
Yet still the pebble lies
within the waters,
covered over,
present in the depths.

So there are circles
in our lives,
sometimes apparent,
sometimes unseen,
and pebbles tossed or
stones skipped cross the surface,
recently or in a distant past,
that we've forgotten
but remain,

www.judysorumbrown.com
judybrown@aol.com

in waters of our memory
or patterns of our dreams,
or at some deeper level of the soul
where mind's eye cannot see so well
because the water's deep and dark.

There am I with you
for all time, where
you have rested
in my center self,
the ripples of my learning,
loving,
in your presence
still in circles like
the moment that
the pebble dropped
so long ago.

www.judysorumbrown.com
judybrown@aol.com

Blue heron

My kayak
traced the path
of light-drenched lily-pads
toward rising sun.
A great blue heron
stood upon the rock and
silent, watched me pass.

We are just presence,
spirit on the move,
witness to life.
We do not own
the land,
nor those we love.
We simply witness life,
holding its beauty for
a moment in our hearts,
then like the great blue heron,
silent still,
we lift our wings
and we are gone.

www.judysorumbrown.com
judybrown@aol.com

The other way

Always
there tugs at me
the other thread,
the other way.
Always,
I hold both
possibilities
and struggle
to find peace
within.
Always,
there's way
not taken,
at least not for now,
and some sweet grief
at what is given up
by making a
wise choice.

www.judysorumbrown.com
judybrown@aol.com

Always there's
tiny longing,
at not seeing
what's around
that corner
on that street,
where early
dawning light
could lead us.
The other way
is aways there.
And so are we.
Roads we pass by
remain forever
in our hearts;

Life's not so much
a river rushing by
as it is stepping stones,
their surfaces
above the river's flow,
and always there
for us to take,

www.judysorumbrown.com
judybrown@aol.com

another time,
and in the drier seasons,
easier to see
and safer for
our feet.

Still there's a yearning
in this moment
to explore right now
those stepping stones,
a tiny path
that disappears
between the trees
within some dappled wood,
the cobblestones that curve
out of our sight
within some foreign
village that we're
passing through
right now.

My heart says,
"We should live so long
to be those lovers
that we see."
And maybe yearning

www.judysorumbrown.com
judybrown@aol.com

means that it is true:
that we should live
so long, to return
naturally to that
same place and
take the other way.

www.judysorumbrown.com
judybrown@aol.com

Current

You bring me news
of longing
answered
by your presence.

You are the
notice of capacity
I had forgotten
that I have.

Your touching me
is indication
of awakening
from a long, long sleep.

Your generosity
and honesty
have turned the key
to some great door
within my heart,
My spirit hears
the tumblers turn
and it rejoices.

www.judysorumbrown.com
judybrown@aol.com

Rainbows

Rainbows are ours
for noticing,
nothing material there,
simply the light on weather,
a chance occurrence and a miracle,
a sunbeam playing
on the tears of nature,
so are you to me,
a rainbow band of feeling,
arcing, touching earth to earth,
a swing connecting sky with ground,
a chance occurrence never hoped for
or predicted,
noticed with a catch of breath
a moment out of time.

For rainbows, I will stop and stand
in stillness, silence,
never asking that they stay,
but soaking them into my mind and spirit,
tracing them with soul, and
in the holding for an instant only,
live a different life forever,
since they've passed my way.

www.judysorumbrown.com
judybrown@aol.com

If I know this of rainbows
how to understand their presence,
see the blessing and the gift,
why not with you and all you are?
to stand in reverence,
in full appreciation,
laughing at your beauty,
wordless in my joy that you are there before me,
touching earth to earth,
and then as light and water change,
a memory that is mine forever,
to reappear another day,
another place, when tears and light
converge again, and I am still to notice

www.judysorumbrown.com
judybrown@aol.com

Labyrinth

Labyrinth

Now stand I
here before you
in the sacred space
of poetry
to say what I have learned
within the labyrinth
of soul.

www.judysorumbrown.com
judybrown@aol.com

Stuck

I have been stuck
enough times
in my life
when there
was simple path,
with ease,
before my
yet unseeing eyes,
to not make
judgements of another
who can't see
what now seems
obvious to me.

I have been graceless
time and time again
before a universe
that offers gifts,
inviting me to dance,
when I, afraid,
refuse to budge.
I will not judge
your fear
at what yet seems
impossible to you.

www.judysorumbrown.com
judybrown@aol.com

I have been shaken, lost,
unseeing and unable
to move forward
in my life,
despite vitality and health
that reach out everywhere
to draw me close.

There are such times,
such harsh hard lessons
to be won,
a shift in mind or heart
to change the world,
a shift that will not come,
until some dawning light
has bathed the earth
and I awake
and all is new.

I wish such dawn
for each of us;
I know it comes.
I don't know where
or when. I'm glad
we travel side by side
till then.

www.judysorumbrown.com
judybrown@aol.com

Crocuses

The crocuses are coming up.
I think that it's
an early sign of spring.
I smile to myself.

He thinks it one more
sign of global warming,
apocalypse upon us,
his face darkens.

She wants a frozen yogurt cone.
I think it's just exactly
what a ten-year-old would want
after a trying day at school.

He thinks her passion is
unhealthy sugar taste,
rampant consumerism,
and he says so
as he drinks his bourbon
to wind down from
stresses of his work.

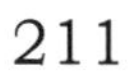

www.judysorumbrown.com
judybrown@aol.com

I come back from a long
and joyous day of work,
awash with energy and thoughts.
He thinks it self-absorption
and a lack of reciprocity.

I feel myself fall silent in response.

We are on different planets
so it seems, two universes
in a single house.

His universe feels toxic
to my soul;
mine must seem
simple and unreal
from where he stands.

He refuses to use fossil fuel
to drive. He walks,
yet in his life
is driven every moment,
every day by demons
that I cannot see.

www.judysorumbrown.com
judybrown@aol.com

I live with paradox, with fears,
with angels of discovery,
with work and colleagues
that I love and trust,
he with the demons of destruction,
disappointment, loss.

It makes a crowded household--
with the jostling angels, demons,
plus the three of us
and one large dog.

I stand at the front door
and look out at the pouring rain.
I still think
crocuses are signs of spring.

www.judysorumbrown.com
judybrown@aol.com

Changing

My life is changing.
I'm alive again,
inhabiting my skin
out to the edges
of myself.

Exhilaration,
fears, contentment
all contend within me,
jostling about.

Yet there seems
room enough
for everyone,
now that
I've come home
to myself.

I've made a choice.
A hard and wrenching one.
There is no
measure to be sure
that it is right,
but just the honesty
to know that it is mine.

www.judysorumbrown.com
judybrown@aol.com

I'll never know
with certainty
the answer to the
question that
emerges from within:
Have I thrown off
the cloth that
covered me,
or have I
saved my soul,
when just enough
and time remained?

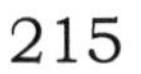

www.judysorumbrown.com
judybrown@aol.com

Wall

It was a wall of anger,
not a wall that kept us safe.

It was a wall of anger,
always reasons for it,
but no room for roses
nor for columbine to grow.

Even when you said
"Excuse me,"
or just "Thank you,"
I felt it like a gauntlet,
catching me across my face,
leaving my cheek red,
burning, like a threat,
or confirmation
of some dreaded truth,
a diagnosis of a terminal disease,
delivered quick and hard.

And even when I
told you how it hurt,
you thought it funny,
as if my hurt
were evidence of weakness

www.judysorumbrown.com
judybrown@aol.com

or of softness
or a failing on my part.
And I believed
that you were right
and so I told my
heart it was required to ignore
the pain it felt.
And while it could,
it did.

Always there was a reason.
You explained and I could
see how you could see it, plain:
a woman you had loved
had lied or had abused you;
a friend or colleague
had made choices
different from your own
and hurt you in some way;
a child or brother had turned out
not as you wanted him to be,
and grew into a person
you could not hold close
because the world had hurt
you, wounded both of you;
the deaths came as they often do
and you felt singled out,
affronted by the world.

www.judysorumbrown.com
judybrown@aol.com

This week I saw a father
with a little girl
waiting to board
a flight delayed.
He sat exhausted
yet relaxed,
upon the floor
with back to wall.
She sat between his legs
and played relaxed and safe.

In all those years
when I was so alone with you,
I never saw you sit like that
and hold us, like a soft
protective wall within which
we could play.

I felt myself begin to cry.
I knew just why the tears
appeared. It was the grief
for something I had longed for,
some sweet part of life denied.

www.judysorumbrown.com
judybrown@aol.com

Forgiveness

Forgiveness
is a tough
requirement,
not that I don't want
to forgive,
but tough because
it means acknowledging
that what he did
was natural to him,
a destiny of sorts.

Undoubtedly, it was
a blindness to my needs
and who I was,
but it was caused
by who he is,
not by some
great and evil
part of him
that I'd not seen before.

It means forgiving
and accepting,
letting be,
giving up judging

www.judysorumbrown.com
judybrown@aol.com

of myself or him.
It means
looking both backwards
and ahead to the
complexity within our lives,
our gifts, our faults,
the pair we were--
just looking at the truth
as one by nature turns ones face
toward the sunshine of a fact.

We were.
He is.
I am.
And I forgive.

I set aside my need
to understand
and analyze.
That need is rooted,
I suspect,
within some thought,
that if I understood,
I could adjust myself or him
to make the marriage work,
or I could change him
so that we'd survive,
a pair.

www.judysorumbrown.com
judybrown@aol.com

God made us as we are,
a raspy fit. When I
forgive us both,
I honor that,
and let us both
be free
to live,
yet once again.

www.judysorumbrown.com
judybrown@aol.com

Morning Glory

The air is thick.
A hurricane
is on its way.
My day is clogged
with errands,
all the overgrowing
details of a life.
I have just five short minutes
set aside to walk the dog.
Yet in those moments
I am suddenly aware
of how the weed-like vines
that clog the woods
have taken flower,
with blooms like little trumpets,
small white morning glories,
growing wild,
with such surprise,
within the woods.

Perhaps my day
will yet unfold as they have,
sprawling sheer beauty,
unexpectedly,
upon my path.

www.judysorumbrown.com
judybrown@aol.com

Prayer

A prayer is not
a pleading
but acknowledging
the presence
in our lives
of just exactly
what we need.

It is a "thank you"
not a "please."
It is commitment
to take over
from the hand
of nature
or of God,
the gardening,
the nurturing
of that which is
most dear.

www.judysorumbrown.com
judybrown@aol.com

It is acceptance
of the gifts
we're given
generously,
a seeing what
lies right
before our eyes,
the bounty of
a generous world.

It is a reaching
out to touch
the presence of
the dream
we hold.

Moonlight in Michigan

In Michigan in moonlight
when the snow is deep,
the fields stretch like an
undulating moonlit sea
in all directions,
an ocean of white snowy
iridescence, dark and light at once,
the dunes and hills
like waves upon
an ocean.

Thus in the black of night
you can still see vast stretches
of the land, as if the fields
were glowing, pouring out their light.

Of course we know it's just reflection of the
moonlight on the snow.
But even so there seems much more to it than that,
as if the moon by looking down,
by being present,
taps a hidden light, a beauty
lying fallow in the hills and fields,
which at the touch of moonlight on the snow,
is brought to life.

www.judysorumbrown.com
judybrown@aol.com

Love is like that, it seems.
When we are loved, we feel the way
the fields do in the moonlight,
as if by mystery,
some moonlight in our lives,
we are transformed.

Perhaps we say in moments
of more sense, of practicality,
moments of daylight,
that all this glow has not to do with us.
It is the presence of the other
that makes such a difference.
And yet the beauty's ours,
elicited by moonlight of a different sort
within our lives.

So love transforms
by touching surfaces and planes
that have been there and always--
yet have seemed plain, uninteresting,
have never seemed like this,
have never glowed before with this strange light.
So love transforms by noticing,
by shining and illuminating, bringing forth
some hidden inner light and beauty,
an iridescence like a chemistry or
sensed connection, like a silent

www.judysorumbrown.com
judybrown@aol.com

touch upon our inner being,
a touch that starts outside us
but which draws our inner light,
a light in daylight that is
never seen, is not perceivable.

In daylight those same
hills and fields
in Michigan
look plain,
uninteresting,
a stalk of weed or grass
protruding through
the grainy snow.

But moonlight changes everything
and unexpectedly
makes magic everywhere,
a dazzling light within
the darkest night
that happens only
in the midst of winter
when the snow is deep
and moonlight reigns
across the hills and dunes.

www.judysorumbrown.com
judybrown@aol.com

Sugar

Connection,
lasting peace
and love
come not
in grasping
after them,
in seeking, chasing,
running after,
but in being,
in the sitting
with our need
in silence
and compassion
for ourselves
and for the longing
and the want.

They are the sweetness
that comes after being
who we are in solitude,
and silence,
and from knowing
we are living without that
for which we long
with such a thirst.

www.judysorumbrown.com
judybrown@aol.com

They are like maple sugar that
comes after all the
hard and sticky work
of tapping maple trees,
the lugging of the slopping
pails through heavy corn snow,
all the hours within the close heat
of the sugar camp,
hours spent at stirring,
so the final sweet
has not a taste of burn.

Peace,
passion,
heart connection,
meetings of the soul
are all like that--
something remaining
after all the work is done--
the hard work of just being human,
living with our failures and integrity,
with pain and loneliness
and fear and longing and with all
the cumbersome and weighty and
exhausting parts of being human
and of caring for oneself and for the world.

www.judysorumbrown.com
judybrown@aol.com

Then comes the sugar finally,
the sweet that lies in crystals
in the sunshine on the snow
for us to taste with laughter
and with joy, as if it had been
easy, which of course,
it was.

www.judysorumbrown.com
judybrown@aol.com

A Poet's heart

"A poet's heart
is never broken,"
so she said. I
knew it to
be true,
this message
of the poet's heart,
which only grows
from life,
no matter what
the path.

The poet's heart
weaves words and pain
and joy into a tapestry,
some beauty,
or a generous shawl
to warm ones self,
or baskets to
hold bread and
homemade rolls,

www.judysorumbrown.com
judybrown@aol.com

or subtle understanding
of the paradox of life,
all woven like fine
fishing net
within which
one can catch
a falling star.

A poet's heart
when caught
by either grief or joy
bends to the loom
of words
and thus is whole
again.

www.judysorumbrown.com
judybrown@aol.com

All who Wander

Rebirth

And we will sell no more
Of our eternity
In payment for dead dreams,
For denial of our losses,
But we will speak of loss
And of rebirth,
And we will treasure
Gifts which are our own.

The time of this travail has passed,
And when another comes,
We will recall,
As if from ancient tribal story
That which we have come to know.

And when the cost of our belonging
Is denial of an older truth,
When we're required
To set aside that which we've learned
Through fire, to be true,
We will then recognize
This is no longer as we hoped,
The circle of our spirit,

www.judysorumbrown.com
judybrown@aol.com

And with deep sadness and necessity
We will then turn our face
Once more toward the path
And journey on until we come
To that new place
Where our true story
Can be spoken
Around yet another tribal fire.

This know we
Now and always.
Let the earth
Remind us
When the storms
Around us
Overwhelm
The tiny, still
Voice of truth within.

www.judysorumbrown.com
judybrown@aol.com

Recluse

Phone messages pour in,
I Write. I write.
A recluse newly formed,
still soft in secret yearning
for the quiet self uncovered here
Within the pages of my work

I cover ears
and board the windows
of myself,
and tape the doorbell over
to keep the world at bay
a while longer - just a while.

Knowing that the moment
cannot last forever
and too selfish to awake
from solitude
and stretch into the day
to come.

www.judysorumbrown.com
judybrown@aol.com

All who wander are not lost

All who wander
Are not lost;
And all who
Return home
Are not yet
Finished with
Their life.
Some wander
To uncover
Something central
To their heart.
Others come home
In order to explore
The mystery,
Not even knowing
That they do,
Simply remaining
True to some
Unerring longing,
Circling and circling
Back to where
They once began,
And where they now,
Belong.

www.judysorumbrown.com
judybrown@aol.com

I've grown lazy

I've grown lazy
Living this way,
Learning to listen
To myself,
Feeling my
Body's rhythms,
My pulse,
My life.

I took
A Sunday
Nap
Today
Just
Because
It felt
Good.

I have run away.
I may never
Come back.

www.judysorumbrown.com
judybrown@aol.com

I don't know what I'm doing

I don't know
What I'm doing,
He said quietly.

Neither do I.

It's good to hear
Another say
Those words
And hear my own reply:

Neither do I.

I've let go
Of the certainty
And settled
Into mystery
And life.

Some matters
Are unfathomable.

www.judysorumbrown.com
judybrown@aol.com

Some currents
Carry us
Without our even
Thinking of their source,
Without our
Asking of their
Course,
Their path,
Their goal.

www.judysorumbrown.com
judybrown@aol.com

Summer sabbatical

I ran away
From home,
From all
The lists
Of things
Undone.
I called it
A sabbatical,
But I had
Run away.
I took off
For some place
Unknown,
For parts unknown,
Of self.
And every stop
I made along the way
Was coming
Home.

www.judysorumbrown.com
judybrown@aol.com

Rabbit sneeze

I heard a rabbit sneeze
While I was walking
Yesterday.
Off to my right,
Out of my sight,
It stopped me
In my tracks.
I knew instinctively
What I had heard,
Even before
I saw her
Scurry off
Into the trees.

My sense of humor
Wondered if
Her sneeze was allergy
To me, the way some
Humans sneeze near
Rabbit fur.

But then a quieter part of me
Thought differently:
Perhaps this simply was

www.judysorumbrown.com
judybrown@aol.com

A natural early morning
Rabbit sneeze
That I would usually
Be too busy,
Anxious and distracted,
To perceive.

But not today.

Today I am
Sufficiently aware
And moving slow enough
To hear a rabbit sneeze.

Achoo.

Bless you.

www.judysorumbrown.com
judybrown@aol.com

Rabbit sneezes and bird safety

I told a friend
About the rabbit sneezing.

She is the kind of
Friend who understands
And doesn't think me
Daffy that the sound
Of rabbit sneezing
Is worth mentioning.

She listened quietly
About the sneeze,
And then out of
The silence she said this:

"I've noticed that
there is a
certain speed
(though somewhat
slower than the
law allows
upon my
rural roads)
below which,
if I drive that speed,
day in,

www.judysorumbrown.com
judybrown@aol.com

day out,
the birds
avoid my car,
and none are killed
as I drive by.
And so
I've taken
to that speed
quite naturally
and year by year
I notice
the results."

So with the rabbit sneeze,
I thought.
I could be walking faster
With my mind at work
Out in the world
And miss
The subtle sound
Of rabbit sneezing,
Just as she could
Arrive where she
Is headed, earlier.

www.judysorumbrown.com
judybrown@aol.com

But now and then
Something alive dies
At those speeds.
Now and again,
Something is lost.

www.judysorumbrown.com
judybrown@aol.com

Ten thousand years ago

Ten thousand years ago
This beach was like it is today.
Before the Europeans,
Maybe even before tribes,
There were these sand expanses
And the ragged bluffs,
The breathing of the waves,
The islands, Manitou and Fox,
The distant promontories
That have western names now:
Whaleback and Pyramid Point.
All stood like this,
The vast expanse,
Completely,
Absolutely desolate
And beautiful.
Today, bundled against
The winter wind,
I walk alone toward
The north, I walk a
Steady pace an hour,

www.judysorumbrown.com
judybrown@aol.com

Then turning back, I
Walk another hour.
In all that time,
In all that space,
I see no other human face,
Nor any footprint,
Nor any sign of human habitation,
Only the waves,
The light, the sand,
The rocks,
Only the solitude
Of God,
Only the Spirit
Of this place.

www.judysorumbrown.com
judybrown@aol.com

Budget resolution

Sometimes the fear
That there won't be enough
Can freeze my heart
And I can't hear
Your voice
Calling to me
In human ways—
And missing wealth,
Or so I think,
Of one kind,
I then squander
An abundance
That the world
Now offers us.

I make a declaration
To myself, to you:
I wish to use
The signal
That the dollars
Are quite tight,
To open up my heart
To that which flows
Quite naturally:

www.judysorumbrown.com
judybrown@aol.com

Human connection,
Life, beauty,
The satisfaction
Of the work well done,
A moment's noticing,
Appreciation of your gifts,
An honest conversation,
Attention to what matters most.

I want to live
These days
Embodying this simple truth:
The dollars may be tight
But I am free
To open up
My heart.

www.judysorumbrown.com
judybrown@aol.com

Eaglet

She is "damp"
She says,
Coming out of
The shell of
Role expectations,
Responding to
Her soul.
She is a
Mountain person,
The peaks, the firs
Are hers.
Newly hatched,
Like an eaglet
On a crag-like outcropping,
She says she feels
Damp yet,
Unfinished,
Becoming herself
In the place
Where she
Is meant to be,

www.judysorumbrown.com
judybrown@aol.com

Days yet
From having any clue
What she's to do,
Or what her yet
Unstrengthened wings
Are for,
And how she is--
In this place and time--
To soar.

www.judysorumbrown.com
judybrown@aol.com

The universe

The universe
Offers its gifts
Shyly and quietly.
And we in brazen
Busyness thoughtlessly
Brush them to the side,
Unseeing in the rush
That has become
Our lives.

Try silence then,
And practice
Small contentedness.

Perhaps within that
Practice newly learned,
The shy gifts
Will emerge
Into the open space of life,
As does a fawn
Who tentatively steps into a glen,
Or kittens who begin
Quite playfully to tumble
From beneath
The front step of our life.

www.judysorumbrown.com
judybrown@aol.com

The gifts of life
Are hiding yet and
Will become quite evident
When we can
Give them time
And space
Within which
To emerge.

www.judysorumbrown.com
judybrown@aol.com

Too soon

Too soon,
Too soon,
The liminal
Moments
Dissolve
Into movement,
Into thoughts
And lists
And bags to
Be readied
For some trip,
When we
Are ever
Already
Here.

www.judysorumbrown.com
judybrown@aol.com

Watching geese

I'm watching
Geese a lot
These days—
The energy
It takes
For them
To get airborne—
The burst of action
When they
Lift off of our creek,
No longer floating
But now flying—
Fighting their way
Toward the sky—
What causes them
To want
To give up floating
With its ease,
For flight?

Connections

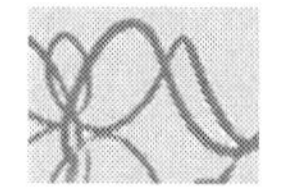

Cornstalks

Cornstalks stand uncut
In warm November winds
Like slender Swedish women
Facing into autumn breezes,
White blond shocks of hair
Streaming behind them,
As they all stare west,
Row upon row of ghostlike
Beauties, silent, saying nothing
To the passing crow, or us,
But keeping their own counsel,
Looking toward the winter night
And cold so soon to come.

www.judysorumbrown.com
judybrown@aol.com

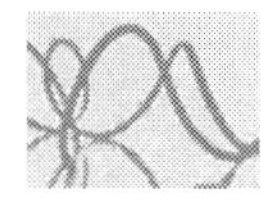

Quilts and carvings

Yesterday a friend said
that to read the poems
draws a sigh of recognition:
"Yes . . . that's it."
And comfort
from the knowing
we are not alone
in pain or in elation,
but that there's
company among us,
someone somewhere
spinning out the words
that match the silent anguish
and intensity of life.

Like knowing
there are women out there
quilting somewhere in small towns,
piecing together squares
of passion and of quandaries,
the inconsolables of life.

Like knowing men in villages
still whittle now and then
with jackknives turned away,
handing little figures to children

www.judysorumbrown.com
judybrown@aol.com

to play games with
or to rub smooth deep in pockets,
or to stand as guardians on the window sill
those long cold winter nights.

We are all wordless
in the deep wells of our lives.

The poems breathe our lives,
they say our words,
and give us space to nod
a mute and grateful "yes"
to that we recognize as ours
so we can feel it,
know it deeper, deeper still,
within our souls,

as if we finger tiny carvings
from a stranger,
or wrap ourselves
in quilts that other women make
in wordless silence
stitching by the candlelight
alone, in silence that is ours.

www.judysorumbrown.com
judybrown@aol.com

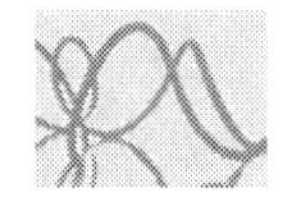

Water's Edge

She told me she was walking on the beach
In preparation for the funeral,
The ending of a period in her life,
The closing of a door to work
That had been heart and soul,
So she could turn her heart
To something new emerging in her life,
A different dream that called her now.

I noticed as she spoke
How often I have felt the need
To bury what once was
Main stream in my life,
In order to be free to turn my face
And go where I must go.
And as she spoke,
I realized the water has a different
Sense of ending and of change.

The water knows
A river can diverge
Around an island,
And become two rivers
For a while,
Or in a delta

www.judysorumbrown.com
judybrown@aol.com

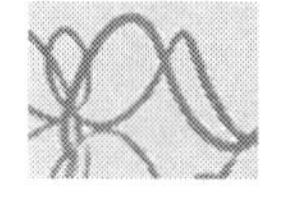

Fan into a handful of small streams,
And still meet ocean's edge.

The water knows
The waves that touch
The shore define a meeting point
Of two realities,
The sand with water's tracings
And the water with its
Breathing in and out,
As if the land
Is how our life once was
And water is baptism
To the new.

They touch each other gently,
Almost kissing, in a kind caress, in quiet,
Not contending and not closing doors,
But standing as two different realities,
One sand and solid,
One shaped out of quiet waves
That creep up to the beach and then recede,
Each a reality of an eternity, and yet a threshold
Which we beach walkers can trace
Between the past and that fresh future
Which we feel as ocean's breeze upon our cheeks.

www.judysorumbrown.com
judybrown@aol.com

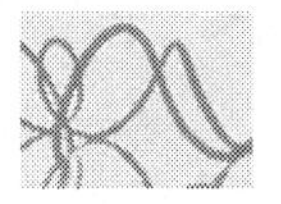

It doesn't need a funeral, nor a burial,
But rather transformation
From the old
To that emerging in our lives.
It just needs walking
At the water's edge,
Perhaps alone,
Perhaps together,
But in a silence,
As if we're tracing
Miles of threshold
Of a door wide open to us all.

www.judysorumbrown.com
judybrown@aol.com

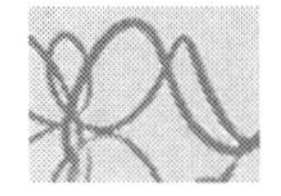

Awake

Who woke me up at two a.m.?
Who among us was
awake, or worried?
Who among us was
drawn deeply into
dreams and pulled me
from my sleep to join
the reverie? Who also
woke and lay with eyes
first closed, and then
wide open, wondering?

Which of us also put on
coffee, and stepped out of doors
under the stars in darkness,
drinking in the night?

Were you there, too, with me?
Or did I, rising unexpectedly
so early with this brew of
dreams and hopes and human fears
drag you from slumber,
pull you to feet
still reaching for their balance
in the dark,

www.judysorumbrown.com
judybrown@aol.com

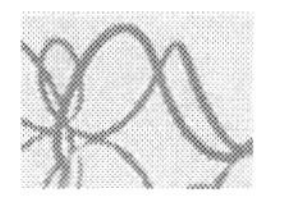

and like me fumbling
for shoes and clothing, wondering
why sleep had fled
so suddenly
to leave you with the
gift of night and time alone,
in solitude,
a symmetry of solitudes
we share, perhaps unknowing
or at the very least
unspoken in the sharing?

Who among us, somewhere on this globe
is with me in the wondering dialogue
of time and timelessness,
of how we find and feel essential links
for which the words fail,
for which a laugh, or smile, or sudden silence,
is the echo or reverberation
of a deeper tone,
to which we tune our lives,
in silent solitude
we share in darkest hours
and at the dawn?

www.judysorumbrown.com
judybrown@aol.com

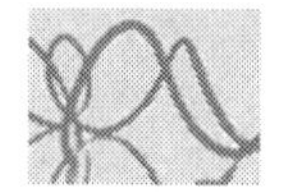

Center

The pain
I hold
deep in
my center
is not mine
to hold.

It is
the key
to opening
a door,
to cleansing
of my spirit house.

It is
not generosity,
nor deep
responsibility,
to hold it tight
within my gut.

It is,
in truth,
unwillingness
to live.

www.judysorumbrown.com
judybrown@aol.com

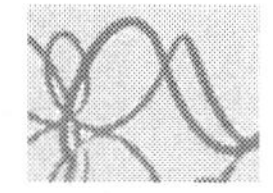

Bullet points

Bullet points
about a life,
the bottom line.

What would they be?

•We have capacity
to build connections
across space
and time.

•We surprise ourselves
and one another
with capacities
unknown.

•We most resist
that which
we most
are drawn to learn.

•No one lives forever.

www.judysorumbrown.com
judybrown@aol.com

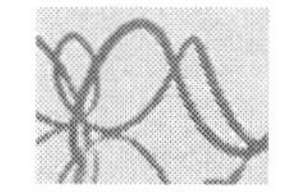

•Our choices
in how we live
our lives may help
us die our deaths.

•When there's no longer
doing we can do,
just being is enough.

•Perhaps it
always was.

•Sometimes,
the time for being
and not doing
comes much sooner
than we think.

www.judysorumbrown.com
judybrown@aol.com

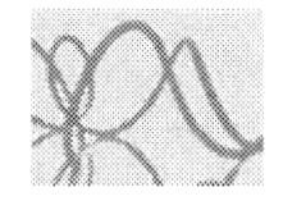

Not here

Today I'll go out to the
grocery store and buy
a roast for Christmas Eve,
and think about my mother
who isn't here
and used to fix the roast.

And when I take a walk
out in the snow,
I'll think of Dad, now
dead three years,
and how his boots
crunched in the snow
when we walked into town
for exercise
after our Christmas feast.

And even when they
still were here with me,
cooking, and walking,
I would think with loneliness
of my new love and feel an ache
of emptiness,
because he was at home
at Christmas time,

www.judysorumbrown.com
judybrown@aol.com

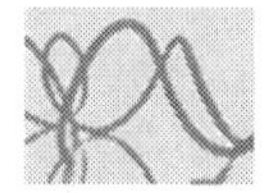

as I was, and not anywhere
where I could really talk
with him, not sitting at my
side at dinner or not walking
with us down the road to town.

And I would listen to the surface
of the words we said or left unsaid
at dinner time, and I would long for Uncle Tom
who half a continent away I knew
would pull me to his side to have
a conversation about life and death,
and dreams, reincarnation, poetry,
the rich stuff that we hide
deep, deep within, and never bring
to life as we are passing the potatoes.
The holidays seem home to
those not here, somehow,
as if they are all touching me on spirit shoulder,
tugging at my sleeve as I am cooking, talking,
spirits saying to me "Listen to me now",
and thus distracting me from other talk
and listening that I am in the middle of,
right here, right now,
pulling me out of my present life
and into lonely silent spaces
where I now go to hear their urgent
whispers, even though they are not here.

www.judysorumbrown.com
judybrown@aol.com

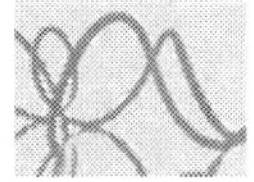

Even you, I find within that
space they make.
You who make my
daily life so rich,
but on the weekends and on holidays,
time with our separate lives,
you too evaporate
like morning mist
that I can't capture
in my grasping hands,
you disappear,
as if you'd climbed down steps
into a basement
and then closed the door, and tight,
so I can't hear you any more.
You disappear like that.
And then you reappear again,
among the spirits who have
shaped my spirit life and who can't seem
to let me live the present simply on the surface
of my life. You reappear with them,
those apparitions of the holidays,
another love out of dimensions of my life
not here right now within this kitchen space,
a piece out of my puzzle heart,
who shapes my holidays by joining forces
with those others whom I love
who are not here.

www.judysorumbrown.com
judybrown@aol.com

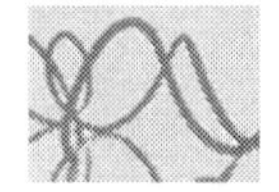

Sleeping child

Sleeping child,
I long for you
To wake,
To snuggle on my lap,
To start the day.

And I am
Grateful for
Your sleep,
The gift of
Silence,
Time to write,
To know myself.

A strange umbilical
Thus links us still,
The knowing you
And knowing me,
The holding you
In such a way
That there is space
To hold myself
As well,
A birthing
Never finished,
Still in process,

www.judysorumbrown.com
judybrown@aol.com

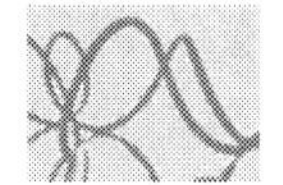

As I breathe
And write
And still,
You sleep.

www.judysorumbrown.com
judybrown@aol.com

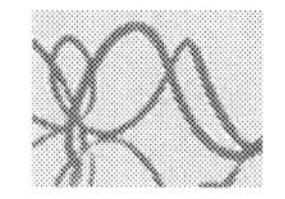

Strangers

We start the time together
Strangers, and end up friends.
I start out wondering
Who you might be
And end up loving you
For all your beauty, energy,
Confusion, for the soft
And human spots,
For edges rough and clear
That speak your heart.

Work shouldn't be like this,
The world would say.
Work's clear objective stuff,
No matter of the heart.
It doesn't seem to work
That way for me.
Whenever work has craft
And skill and artistry,
My heart's right in there
In the middle of it all.
Whenever work is gloriously fun
Or deeply troublesome,

www.judysorumbrown.com
judybrown@aol.com

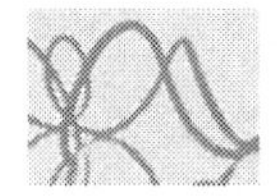

My heart wades in
And drags me with it,
Never asking how I like the water,
Or even if I swim at all.

Whenever work's worth doing,
None of me can stay behind.
And so we start out strangers
And I end up loving you.

www.judysorumbrown.com
judybrown@aol.com

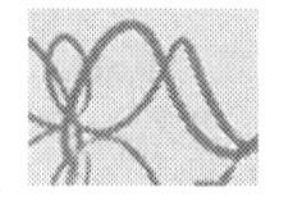

Daughter

Daughter isn't some
relationship. Daughter
is my bone, my blood,
my heart. Daughter
isn't yet another
generation. Daughter
is my essence poured
into the years to come.
Daughter isn't someone
I am raising, she is
mother-daughter bonds
to come, and layers of
those bonds that lie
behind us in the dust
of generations past.
Daughter is the haunting
call of all my choices,
dreams and passions,
calling out again, right now,
my child-like self dancing again
at water's edge at sunset,
walking the stone walls by the sea,
finding her way
while with a steadying hand
I walk beside.

www.judysorumbrown.com
judybrown@aol.com

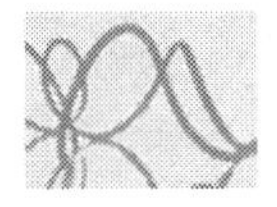

Granite

She said in meeting you
she realized the bond I felt with you
was natural,
and unavoidable.
It was, she said,
as if in meeting you,
she'd met the other half of me,
as if despite our surface differences
there is some core,
where we are kin,
come from a common stock,
grown from a single root
far under ground.

It made me wonder
if there is an ancient god
somewhere, who carves us
out of granite bounders,
each of us,
and where the boulder is
expecially large,
that diety carves two,
each with a surface
that is different,
but with a core that is the same.

www.judysorumbrown.com
judybrown@aol.com

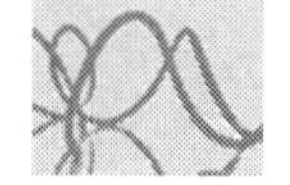

And then the carver
scatters us about the globe
unknown to one another,
and notes with pleasure,
when by serendipity we're thrown
upon each other's path.

And that creator
with a sense of humor
watches as we mortals
feel some bond
which has no source
that we can see.
Baffled at reasons
we have come to sense such link,
we journey side by side,
completely unaware
that we are carved
out of a single granite rock
that, split asunder long ago,
now finds its whole
in accidental meeting,
in a friendship
that is rock
and root
at once.

www.judysorumbrown.com
judybrown@aol.com

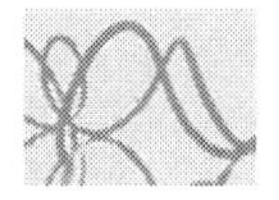

Hymns

You said with anger
that they'd changed the hymnal,
taken out the old time hymns
your grandmother had sung,
erased them. And in doing so
it seems they took a part
of her away from you.

Why would they do a thing like that?
You carried her in song.
They must not know.

They must think songs are just
a printed thing upon the page.
And not the footprints of the memories
of those we love, singing an old time tune.

If they had known that such was true of hymns,
they would just add the new ones at the back,
or maybe print the hymnals with the last pages
a simple white, so new hymns could be added to
the old without changing a thing.

www.judysorumbrown.com
judybrown@aol.com

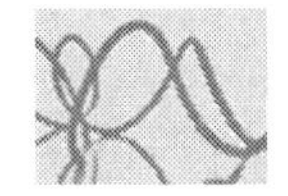

They wouldn't have to take some out
to add the new, as now they do,
as if the hymns, the songs, the words
are just spare parts,
exchangeable one for the other
like spark plugs or light bulbs,
in machines that never know
what comes and goes.

I think the hymns are like
a hammer that my father held,
his old canoe, his shirt;
they carry spirit like a totem does.
So we must set about
to find old hymnals
to reclaim the ones we love,
or sing the songs ourselves
so they are known.

Like troubadours who carry stories
in a song, from place to place,
we thus repair the damage that's been done,
when in a fascination with the new,
they take the old songs out of books,
and with them take the heart of
those we love and all the memories
we carried there in pages worn,
in times recalled,

www.judysorumbrown.com
judybrown@aol.com

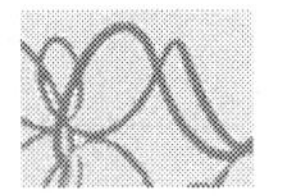

in songs they sang, we sang with them,
in days now long ago.

www.judysorumbrown.com
judybrown@aol.com

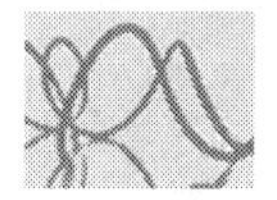

Now II

Our past and future
pull us from
the moment
were we live our lives,
the now in which we breathe
and love and cry.

Eternity is made
up of such sacred times,
the moments, slivered,
that run deep,
down, down
into the soul
or way out to the edges
of a universe
we cannot see
with just the naked eye,
but with the naked heart.

www.judysorumbrown.com
judybrown@aol.com

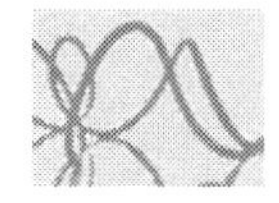

Wind II

The wind is blowing.
Everything is moving but the stars
and they are brilliant, clear.

I cannot be unmoving in
the face of all the wind.
It sounds like autumn coming
earlier than we expect,
the rustle of the wind in
Aspens, building, ebbing,
like a tide, or like the
breathing of the universe.

Nothing is lost forever
if we come to think
in ways yet large enough
to hold it all.
The things that burn or die
are dust still blowing in the wind.
Out on a night like this
they ride the waves,
and so do we,
when we are dying
and still being
born again.

www.judysorumbrown.com
judybrown@aol.com

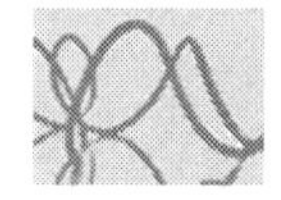

Turning point II

One day I kayaked in the fog at dusk,
and way across the pond
I found myself nearing the shore,
facing a great dead tree,
stark in mid-summer,
without leaves.

Two eagles rested at its top,
unmoving as I floated there below,
and after while,
as if with great deliberation,
first one, and then the next,
took flight.

They flew away not as a pair.
Each went a separate way.
The second one set course north up the pond
and then was lost from sight within
the massive oaks that hang o'er water's edge.

It was a way that seemed to call
and so I went that way myself at easy pace,
and found to my surprise
a trio of great loons
paddling in silence in the fog.

www.judysorumbrown.com
judybrown@aol.com

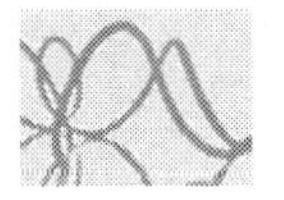

They paddled straight toward me.
I now was resting, floating,
curious as they seemed to be.
They paddled til I was within
their midst and held me there,
making a clucking sound,
a welcome so it seemed,
no hint of their great mournful cry,
just quiet sounds.

They didn't dive.
They stayed with me
as if to welcome me
and hold me in their midst.
After a while
we went our separate ways,
the loons and I.
And as I crossed the pond
the eagle swept o'erhead
as in salute.

www.judysorumbrown.com
judybrown@aol.com

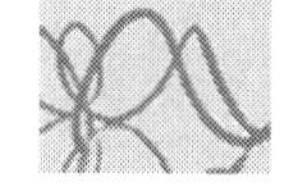

I paddled home in darkness.
The fog was gone,
the stars emerging
from the deepening blue.
I sensed a turning point
and as my life unfolded,
it was true.

www.judysorumbrown.com
judybrown@aol.com

Roger's House

Rascals

"Rascals" he called the guys at work.
A funny word, of love and humor,
like a father talks about a child
he loves, one who is small enough
to be enjoyed with mud on face.

Perhaps we need to be that way
with one another when we end up
in the mud and stuck. Not to
belittle what the other's done,
no matter how frustrating it may be,
but rather see the rascally face
that looks to us for guidance
in the mess, and wade right
in to help the rascal out.

www.judysorumbrown.com
judybrown@aol.com

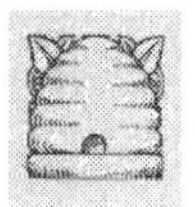

Trilliums

He said to me
That sometimes
When he's in the woods
In springtime,
And the trilliums are blooming,
He disappears.
Completely.
He is gone
Into the whole of things,
Lost
In the universe
Of which he is
A breathing part.
Gone home.

www.judysorumbrown.com
judybrown@aol.com

Connection

It is
A massive place
And old,
Built for
Another time
And place,
Yet working still.

A place where people
Work the presses,
Handle steel,
Make coils of rods,
Shape car parts,
Pass them on,
One to the next.

If you want
To be heard
Above the din,
You have to touch
Each other,

www.judysorumbrown.com
judybrown@aol.com

Standing very close,
Leaning into words near lost
Within the vastness
Of the place.

One man,
Explaining what he did,
With pride,
Touched me
To draw me near
So I could hear.

Touched me,
This stranger did.
I heard his
Every word.

www.judysorumbrown.com
judybrown@aol.com

Leonardo

If I read
My poetry
Out loud,
In public
Am I then
A poet?
Not a farmer,
Not a teacher,
Not a focused
Manager or
Leader?

But a poet?

Maybe you are
Leonardo,
He said,
Quietly.

www.judysorumbrown.com
judybrown@aol.com

It doesn't matter

It doesn't matter
how I dress
or if I'm perfect
and my life
is as I wanted it
to be. It only
matters that I'm
present to you,
as you are right now,
and to myself.
Alive.

It doesn't matter
what I say,
or that I tell
you everything
I think I know.
It only matters
that I listen
to your heart
beneath your words.

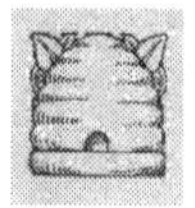

It doesn't matter
that at other times,
I have screwed up a
perfect possibility;
it only matters
that I hold
eternity with you
in this one moment,
and I know it's so.

It only matters that I see
the grace in this one gritty
time within our lives,
the way the light
falls on a field at dusk,
the flight of birds,
the cricket sounds.

That only matters
to eternity and me.

www.judysorumbrown.com
judybrown@aol.com

Swissair flight 111

Swiss watch, Swissair,
both mean reliability,
assurance, safety, life.
The experts still are wondering
what happened to that Swissair flight,
what dropped those living,
breathing people to a watery grave.
It was Swissair, no safer way to fly.

Maybe our science
will reveal the cause
and maybe not.

Till then, and after then as well,
we're left to ponder how
the safest things in life
are not infallible.

I lived part of that story years ago,
a flight with engine lost,
so heavy that we couldn't land,
and so we passed an hour in silence,
in the air far west of London,
pouring jet fuel over ocean waves,
and then we turned,

www.judysorumbrown.com
judybrown@aol.com

a wide and careful arc,
headed for landing,
braced for impact.
But we lived.

It was a different airline,
world class, but now gone, extinct,
its logo a collector's item.
And our plane load of just such
living breathing folks,
we made it, didn't face our end,
on that one day, decades ago.
I had forgotten how it felt
to make that flight,
to turn that careful arc,
to land alive,
til they did not.

Time's Elastic

Time's elastic edge
stretches, reworks,
arranges life,
the memories and intuitions
pulled in patterned
loops and weavings,
in a dynamic tapestry
of images, experience,
memories and dreams
all interlinked.

I live that tapestry.
I'm six again,
lying beneath the trees,
and as my daughter Meg
has written, "I am drunk on sky"
and then quite instantly
I'm in the power of
our loving, yours and mine,
and then the winds of time blow,
suddenly I'm here
within this space,
writing a poem
at on this granite countertop.

www.judysorumbrown.com
judybrown@aol.com

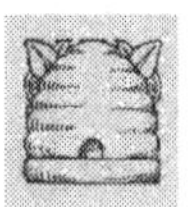

It seems
it's true
that all is one,
and one is all:
the time, the loving
and the call.

www.judysorumbrown.com
judybrown@aol.com

Truth

In this place,
last time,
someone died,
because
he pushed himself
too hard.
True,
he was on a high,
but he is dead.
He didn't speak
the truth
of his condition.
And we pretended
not to know.
Have we now
learned the lesson
we can take
from how he died—
to speak
our truth,
as if
our lives
depend on it?

www.judysorumbrown.com
judybrown@aol.com

Thunder

Heart
roll on
like thunder,
like the weeping,
cooling,
healing
rain.

Let words
seed fields
of life,
where in the
warmer days to come,
the grain
will feed
a world
and flocks
as well.

For now,
just sow
the seeds,
and let
the rain fall
as it will.

www.judysorumbrown.com
judybrown@aol.com

India

He stood in line
behind me
as we waited
for the plane
to the East Coast,
a beautiful young man,
from India, an engineer.

Will he go home?
To India?
He doesn't know.
His college prof, idealist,
Tells him going home is right.
"He hasn't been to India,
my prof," he says.

"How is it there?" I ask.
He smiles but softly,
"It's an experience," he says.
"Things don't work well.
It's an experience," is all he'll say.
"Maybe I'll just stay here.
Maybe."

www.judysorumbrown.com
judybrown@aol.com

"Your family?" I ask.
"They want me to return,
My dad, who didn't take the
fellowship to Princeton,
(my grandmother,
convinced him
not to go), he urges my return."

"And you?"
"It would take courage
to return."
"Yes, and quite another kind
to stay. Perhaps you'll know
in time which kind
you want to chose."

"Yes," he says.
Then smiling, as if an afterthought
he says, "And in the meantime,
I enjoy it all, all that I can do here
that isn't possible at home.
I'm playing hockey on a team."
He laughs. "I'm not much good.
It's fun."

www.judysorumbrown.com
judybrown@aol.com

We board the plane,
and at flight's end,
as we are leaving,
I can see him near me,
smiling at me, as he helps
an old and greying woman,
Indian like him,
a stranger struggling with her bag.
We go our separate ways.

And as I watch
him helping her,
I sense
we both will know
which courage
we should choose
when time comes
to decide.

www.judysorumbrown.com
judybrown@aol.com

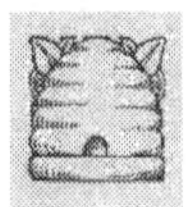

A mourning

I've been a-mourning,
these last months,
a dozen, two or three.
For years, perhaps.

A widow has a sharper
ache, a clearer sense
of just what's lost,
than does a wife
who wakes to find
that what she told
herself was present,
never was, and likely
never will appear.

It is a death of
some fine dream,
thus to awake
to life and pain
at once. A wailing
deep within, at some
sharp loss so wrenching
that there are no words.

www.judysorumbrown.com
judybrown@aol.com

A woman told me once
that no one brings you casseroles
when marriage dies; for
loss of love there's no
expected ritual, for loss
so personal, so painful
and so common it seems trite.

Yet there's a pain
deeper than even this,
I think, and it's to live a lie,
to lie in a relationship
that has lost heart and soul
and to believe that in the name
of deep commitment, it must
be and thus, and for forever more.

That is a loss eternal
and unending,
of the self and truth.

I've turned away
from that great silent, inner loss,
only to live into another,
one more visible,
a semi-public mourning
without funeral, or notice
in the press; a grieving

www.judysorumbrown.com
judybrown@aol.com

reluctantly admitted,
first to myself
and then to others,
of the loss
of what I thought
could not be lost,
but was no longer there.

www.judysorumbrown.com
judybrown@aol.com

Miracles II

God gives us miracles.

I never knew
a miracle
would be a pen.
And paper.
Time and silence.
Dreams and space.

I thought that miracles
would come in big
and fancy, splashy packages.
Some huge surprise.

They come instead
to me in stark simplicity,
in life seen
in periphery,
in tiny things,
in what was there
and all along:
a breath, a song,
a sudden seeing
of the beauty
in my life.

www.judysorumbrown.com
judybrown@aol.com

Songbird

Crows and crickets
now compete for airspace.
In such cacophony,
how do the songbirds
find the space to sing?
How are they heard?
The tiny one from
yesterday, no bigger
than a prune, how does
she get into the symphony
and sing her song?

I guess she just begins
and sings,
and doesn't worry
if we hear,
but hearing herself start
to sing, it's that alone
makes space,
gives her encouragement,
brings forth her song.

www.judysorumbrown.com
judybrown@aol.com

Dense

Dense. That's how
you feel to me.
Just dense.
Like sinew or a rock.
Some moments
I can see
the open heart
at center of
the rock you are,
as if volcano's center
still is vibrant
and alive,
molten and warm.

At other times,
I slam into the surface
of your hardened self.

I wonder
if you too
can sense
as now I do
the difference
between the live
volcano and the
hard, hard rock.

www.judysorumbrown.com
judybrown@aol.com

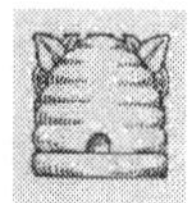

Synchronicity

He said that innocence
was key to seeing
natural openings,
that show us
how completely
we are linked,
We call it synchronicity.

"Yes, innocence is right,"
I thought, "And also love,
and death, and loss so great
it takes our breath away.
And giving into life with joy,
as children do who
fall with glee
into a pile of leaves."

Those moments come
when life grabs us,
smashing the walls
we have constructed
round our soul,
the moments when
we see how life,

www.judysorumbrown.com
judybrown@aol.com

the essence of our self,
is part of something vast
that we once
knew about
and then forgot.
The synchronicity is
present in those moments, too,
when we allow ourselves
to feel the yearning, pain,
impossibility,
and don't give up,
and can't insist,
but sit in dreams
and in the muck
of life,
in calm,
and pain
and joy,
those moments when the
paradox pulls us apart
and opens us up to eternity.

Then we are innocent
able to see
what has been there
to see
right from the start.

www.judysorumbrown.com
judybrown@aol.com

Moment

A poem
is a moment
out of time,
a density
where everything
compresses
into simple words
that hug
the whole
damned thing
so hard
it takes
your breath away,
and won't let go.

www.judysorumbrown.com
judybrown@aol.com

A Deer

I hear an animal outside,
no doubt a deer.
It's large, I'm sure,
the sounds say that.
It is too dark to see,
I only hear,
and can imagine,
from the sounds
of branches clicking,
breaking,
that intruder is a deer.

Sometimes it is too dark
to see, and my
imaginings are fear;
today it's wildlife
I imagine,
not some dreadful thing.

I notice that the difference
between the recognition
and the fear,
lies only in my mind
and in experience:

www.judysorumbrown.com
judybrown@aol.com

I lived, a child, in such
a rural place. I've heard
the sounds of deer
since I began to hear.

So noises here
are comforting,
even when
it is dark,
and nothing
can be seen.

A Leader's Guide to Reflective Practice.

Wooden Boats

I have a brother who builds wooden boats,
Who knows precisely how a board
Can bend or turn, steamed just exactly
Soft enough so he, with help of friends,
Can shape it to the hull.

The knowledge lies as much
Within his sure hands on the plane
As in his head;
It lies in love of wood and grain,
A rough hand resting on the satin
Of the finished deck.

Is there within us each
Such artistry forgotten
In the cruder tasks
The world requires of us,
The faster modern work
That we have
Turned our life to do?

Could we return to more of craft
Within our lives,
And feel the way the grain of wood runs true,
By letting our hands linger
On the product of our artistry?

www.judysorumbrown.com
judybrown@aol.com

Could we recall what we have known
But have forgotten,
The gifts within ourselves,
Each other too,
And thus transform a world
As he and friends do,
Shaping steaming oak boards
Upon the hulls of wooden boats?

Fire (Original version)

What makes a fire burn
is space between the logs,
a breathing space.
Too much of a good thing,
too many logs
packed in too tight
can squelch a fire,
can douse the flames
almost as surely
as a pail of water can.

So building fires
requires tending in a special way,
attention to the wood
as well as to the spaces in between,
so fire can catch, can grow, can breathe,
can build its energy and warmth
which we so need in order
to survive the cold.

We need to practice
building open spaces
just as clearly as we learn
to pile on the logs.

www.judysorumbrown.com
judybrown@aol.com

It's fuel, and absence of the fuel
together, that make fire possible,
let it develop in the way that's
possible when we lay logs in just the
way the fire wants to go.

Then we can watch it as it leaps and plays,
burns down and then flames up
in unexpected ways.

Then we need only lay a log on it
from time to time.
It has a life all of its own,
a beauty that emerges
not where logs are
but where spaces can invite the flames
to burn, to form exquisite
patterns of their own,
their beauty possible
simply because the space is there,
an opening in which the flame
that knows just how it wants
to burn can find its way.

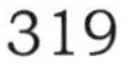

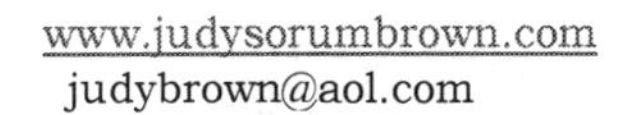
www.judysorumbrown.com
judybrown@aol.com

Stepping Back

Stepping back
Creates the space—
For insight,
Some small flame
Of creativity,
For some new
 sprout
To push through
To the light.
The growth will
Do what's needing to be done;
Our work is to
Create the space

www.judysorumbrown.com
judybrown@aol.com

Life Dictates

"Life dictates much
Of what I do," I thought.
A role,
A should,
An ought,
A not,
A rule,
A discipline,
A job,
A necessary harshness,
Some kind of holding in
And holding on.

Then later on as
We all sat in silence,
I could see I had the
Kernel of a truth,
But had it wrong.
My life, as it turns out,
Does dictate much,
But not the way I meant.

It dictates poetry with
Truth so clear and solid
That it vibrates
Like a tuning fork,

www.judysorumbrown.com
judybrown@aol.com

And as it dictates thus,
Instead of closing ways,
It opens ways, it clears
A path I did not see.

Life dictates much,
Indeed, and doing so
It sets me free.

www.judysorumbrown.com
judybrown@aol.com

Trust equals speed

"Trust equals speed," he said
Explaining why we need
To trust at work. Trust
Lets us move ahead
With lightening speed.
I think he's right.

Yet trust takes time.
It's silent, too,
And meditative in its
Steps. It moves at
Paces that seem slow
And hesitating,
First one foot,
Then the next.

Trust is a dance
Developed over time,
A set of natural steps
Emerging from a bond
Forged from the passion

www.judysorumbrown.com
judybrown@aol.com

That we feel for dreams
We hold in common,
And respect
For all the ways we're not alike,
Both held, the dreams and difference,
Unflinching and aware,
Day after day,
As we work
Side by side.

Trust equals speed.
Yet it is utterly,
Completely still.
Trust is unmoving
And it is the speed
Of light.

www.judysorumbrown.com
judybrown@aol.com

Things as they Are

To live with a full measure of real joy
Seems to require that we
Work with things as they now are,
And at the same time
Speak our hunger for our dreams,
For something well beyond
That which we see.
It means I feel the world
Imperfect, human, flawed,
Myself as well,
And know the vision
That I hold is present
In this moment that I live,
A treasure overshadowed
And not seen because
Not looked for, or not
Trusted, or just lost within
The dark and scary corners
Of the place where we now
Shine the light.

www.judysorumbrown.com
judybrown@aol.com

There is no other way to
Move toward joy, toward grace, vitality,
But to hold dreams
And loose them all at once,
To work with things as they emerge,
Seeing the tiny buds in need
Of time to grow, weeding the
Flat-leaved things that keep
The light from things we love;
Tending the little plants
Needing just light and space
And moisture to grow strong.
Despite my sense that action is
What life demands of me,
There isn't all that much I need to do
To make a space for what I love,
But to acknowledge that I love it.

www.judysorumbrown.com
judybrown@aol.com

Tad Mule

My friend Mary
Has hatched
A whole new
Word: "Tad mule"

It is a little
Notion
That grows up
To be
A stubborn idea.

I have those.

www.judysorumbrown.com
judybrown@aol.com

Cynicism in the Workplace

Cynicism
In the workplace,
Like anger
When a love affair goes sour,
Is about passion disappointed,
About heartache,
About grief.

Dreams dashed
And promises denied
Harden the heart
That planned to offer
Everything,
And now has come
To offer but a wary wondering
And tiny bits
Of reserve energy
Carefully meted
Out.

www.judysorumbrown.com
judybrown@aol.com

Trough

There is a trough in waves,
A low spot
Where horizon disappears
And only sky
And water
Are our company.
And there we lose our way
Unless
We rest, knowing the wave will bring us
To its crest again.
There we may drown
If we let fear
Hold us within its grip and shake us
Side to side,
And leave us flailing, torn, disoriented.

But if we rest there
In the trough,
Are silent,
Being with
The low part of the wave,
Keeping
Our energy and
Noticing the shape of things,
The flow,

www.judysorumbrown.com
judybrown@aol.com

Then time alone
Will bring us to another
Place
Where we can see
Horizon, see the land again,
Regain our sense
Of where
We are,
And where we need to swim.

www.judysorumbrown.com
judybrown@aol.com

Ethics is Wrestling

Ethics
Is wrestling
With life–
The twists,
The sweat,
The strain–
It's not
The high jump
After all,
The race
Well run–
It is the mat
Upon the ground,
And shoulders,
And the
Struggle
To stay free.

Occupation

"Occupation?"
Says the woman,
Laughing,
At the window seat,
As the big jet
Prepares to land
In paradise.
She's helping her
Companion fill out
Immigration forms.
"Occupation?"
"Put 'Lover,' " she says
Laughing once again,
"Put 'International Lover.' "
He laughs, and with an
Accent, rich, adds,
"French Lover."
Laughing,
He fills in
The blank on the form:
"Hairdresser."

www.judysorumbrown.com
judybrown@aol.com

Cirque Du Soleil

When I grew up
The circus
Had the animals
In cages,
The elephants
In lines.

Then even as that scene
Began to trouble me,
Emerged within our lives
A circus of a different kind:
No animals at all,
But humans with trapezes,
Trampolines and bicycles.
Instead of ropes and whips,
There were long flowing sheets
Of ruby-colored silk
From which the
Acrobats could swing.
What saved the animals?
Was it our seeing
What we'd done to them
And feeling bad?

www.judysorumbrown.com
judybrown@aol.com

Or was it
That the beauty
Of a way
Of doing "circus"
So entirely new,
Swept us away,
And saved us from ourselves,
And saved the elephants
And tigers too?

www.judysorumbrown.com
judybrown@aol.com

Seed

Vision is seed,
the thing real
in a form
we don't yet see.

Not that we couldn't
see it if we were
a squirrel,
a worm,
or God.

An acorn is
as real a thing
as is an oak full grown,
a seed precisely like a tree
but in a different shape and time.

In that sense
seeds are possibilities
and certainties at once,
genetic maps of trees,
small promissory notes of
beauty yet to come,
their outward
size and shape still

www.judysorumbrown.com
judybrown@aol.com

bearing no resemblance
to the vast and branching tree
they later will become.

Our dreams and visions
too are absolutely real,
as real as what we now call real,
but they are in a different form,
present within our lives right now,
alive in every breath we take,
yet in a shape we don't perceive
or on a scale that we can't recognize,
unless like squirrels
we dig below the ground.

Or they are with us in a different time,
a time we call the future,
or eternity, or in a dream,
yet just as present and
as grounded as the seed,
and just as surely steward
of a treasure for a time
we call "not now, not yet,"
as is the acorn
with its secret and its promise
held in silence
for the time to come.

www.judysorumbrown.com
judybrown@aol.com

There are countries

There are countries
In our minds,
Whose boundaries
Keep thoughts
From crossing over,
Wondering.
No passports
To be had,
No possibility
Of exploration.

www.judysorumbrown.com
judybrown@aol.com

The Bridge with a Sign

He had found
A bridge,
With a sign:
"Please use
this bridge
to cross."

He wondered aloud
How many times
In his life
He had wandered
On the bank
Of a river of change,
And not seen
Such an obvious sign,
Nor put his
Foot upon the bridge
Before him.

Good Samaritan

The Good Samaritan
Isn't just about
Someone dying
By the roadside.
It's about
Someone lost
In a hallway
In your organization,
And,
Too busy to pause,
You do.

www.judysorumbrown.com
judybrown@aol.com

Life's not a Battle

Life's
Not a battle,
But adventure,
Not a test,
But an
Experiment
We undertake
With curiosity
Because
We want
To know
How something
Works.
'Tis knowing this
As simple fact
Makes all
The difference.

www.judysorumbrown.com
judybrown@aol.com

Competitor

You have
No possible
Competitor in being
Wholly who you are.
In such
A race
As that,
The field
Is completely
Yours.

www.judysorumbrown.com
judybrown@aol.com

Applewood

Apple wood is what I need,
Gnarled apples wood,
Old, beyond growing apples, and not straight
As woodcutters would like,
But limbs of apple trees,
Twisted and perfect for a fire.

A fire builder's view of wood
Is different from the view
Of those who cut and split and stack.

I love the odd shaped ones,
Unlike each other,
Small ones, each unique,
A story in themselves,
So when they're placed upon the fire
They leave a natural space
One to the next,
Because they're crooked,
And not even, not alike.

It's in those spaces grows the fire,
With easy sparking,
Without tending.

www.judysorumbrown.com
judybrown@aol.com

I need to tell him
that the big straight logs,
green wood, will never do.

Give me dry apple wood
From broken, fallen trees.
It's best for fires.

www.judysorumbrown.com
judybrown@aol.com

The circles of our conversation

The circles of our conversation
Help us face each other
And the task before us,
With a hopefulness
We had not known
Until we met.

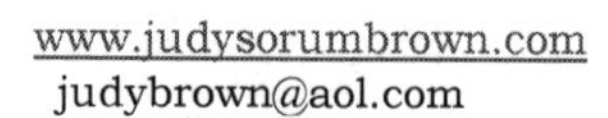
www.judysorumbrown.com
judybrown@aol.com

Dialogue and measurement

"How do you know it works?" he asked
Of dialogue. I said I didn't know.
Like asking if a kiss worked
Or if a hug had done its job.

They say it does.
The listening helps, they say.
But then again, how do they know?
What can you measure of a glance?

If you can't measure it, they say,
Forget it.
Here's what I say to you,
Toss out the yardstick,
And let's value what is true.

www.judysorumbrown.com
judybrown@aol.com

Stop it

Stop it right now.
Stop all the judging, planning,
Stern admonishments
About the task to come.
Just stop it.

For just one moment
Could we breathe it in—
The little victory
Of our work danced
With effortless integrity?

For just one moment
Could we celebrate
And hug each other gleefully
And laugh, and throw a hat
High over head?

For just one moment
Could we close our eyes
In silence, savoring the joy
Of something difficult and beautiful,
Attempted? Done.

www.judysorumbrown.com
judybrown@aol.com

For just one moment could we feel
The deep connection
Built in laboring together,
And in caring for the work
And for each other?

The time will come, too soon,
To plan the next thing,
And to judge the last.

www.judysorumbrown.com
judybrown@aol.com

Seconds

She sells the perfect ones,
the cups and bowls without
a flaw, the ones that
with a potter's eye and hand
she knows will likely never
chip nor break,
will stand the heat and cold,
weather a thousand washings
and remain as new.

The seconds?
Those she keeps and uses,
lives with day to day.
Some have a flaw
that even I can see;
others look perfect
to my untrained eye,
but she's aware
they won't withstand
the challenge
of a stranger's
daily use.

www.judysorumbrown.com
judybrown@aol.com

"Incomplete ideas" she calls
the ones she keeps
just for herself.
"Unfinished thoughts,"
the seconds, plates and bowls,
not flawed but incomplete.

Perhaps it's true for
all of us who craft a thing,
who write a poem,
build a boat,
shape an idea
or an enterprise.

The perfect ones,
the ones that work,
we sell or give away.
We move beyond them,
on to something new.
They pass out of our minds.

www.judysorumbrown.com
judybrown@aol.com

The yet unfinished thoughts,
ideas incomplete,
things that won't work,
we look at every day.
We live more with the
flaws of craft
than with its perfect form.
Perhaps that's why
it's difficult to see
the grace of our own artistry,
to bring to mind the gifts
we've shipped away from us,
to recollect the beauty of
a plate that someone
else can touch
from day to day,
while we ourselves
thrice daily
take our nourishment
from pieces that
we know are flawed.

www.judysorumbrown.com
judybrown@aol.com

A Thin Film

When I
Stare
At the
Moon
Through my
Slightly
Dirty windows,
It seems
To glow.

There is
Pleasure
In the
Softening halo
Of a
Thin film
Of illusion.

www.judysorumbrown.com
judybrown@aol.com

∞

Loon song

Sometimes a solitary loon floats
On the glassy pond at dawn
Just off the cabin's point
In silence.
Across the pond
Another loon cries out.
Then silence.
This one makes no answer.
Listens. Silent. Dives. Appears.
Then floats, head turned.

Why, thus, no answer?
Was the question
To another listener?
Or was it so compelling
That no answer can be made?
Or in the world of loons is
Silence the response of choice,
Of deep respect?

Would that as friends and colleagues
We could recognize that voice,
And listen to the call in silence,
Head turned toward the call,
In pensive silence,
Wondering, respectful.

www.judysorumbrown.com
judybrown@aol.com

Lunch with Alice

He's leaving
The Academy,
He told the Dean.

It seems
He wants
To linger longer
Over lunch
With Alice,
His beloved.

World-renowned
For his intellect,
The Nobel prize in hand,
He's listening
To his heart.

www.judysorumbrown.com
judybrown@aol.com

Stories

When the stories
Begin and we listen,
Really listen
To each other,
We begin
To notice
That we are not
Quite so much the same
As we had thought,
At least
Not in the ways
We thought.
And we are not
So different as we thought,
At least not in the ways
We thought.
And like some
Big old family
Full of odd relatives,
We are all kin,
Befuddled
And beloved.

www.judysorumbrown.com
judybrown@aol.com

Trust

Trust rises and falls
Like a tide.
See now it ebbs,
The shoals are visible,
The waves break
Far from shore.
Then, as is ever true,
We glance away,
Distracted by
Some beauty,
And fail to notice
That the waves upon the sand
Are now
Much closer to our feet.
The tide
Is coming in again.
Who or what
Makes it thus,
This breathing in and out
Of universe,
This feeling love
Give way to fear
And then to love
Again?

www.judysorumbrown.com
judybrown@aol.com

How do I,
Losing faith in you
Or me,
Wait for the tide
To do its work,
Turning,
To then
Transform our world?

www.judysorumbrown.com
judybrown@aol.com

The Pizza Came

The pizza came
But not the rental chairs.
So the tough issues
They were so upset about,
Had to be talked about
One at a time
With folks sitting
Upon the floor,
Informal, pow-wow style,
Listening to one another.
Eating pizza.
Even laughing
Now and then.
They'll meet again
Like that
In two more weeks.
They've found
A whole new world
Together.
If the chairs had come
And not the pizza,
They would have been
In an entirely
Different place.
Providence moves
In strange ways.

www.judysorumbrown.com
judybrown@aol.com

Some Days

Some days
You see the depth
Of distant hills
Because the light
Is touching them
Just so—
And other moments
That detail, perspective,
Is completely lost to view,
And there is nothing
You can do
But just recall
What you've already seen,
Try to remember the detail.
It's the condition
Of the light
That changes all.

www.judysorumbrown.com
judybrown@aol.com

The Sea at Grace Bay

Barefooted

Here
you could
live
barefooted.
Novel
idea.

www.judysorumbrown.com
judybrown@aol.com

Infinite Encounters

The reef,
the waves
that break
across
its sheltering arm,
have no intention,
do no work,
are simply being,
naturally:
the beauty
they create eternally
is born by
infinite encounters
that they do not
think about,
nor plan.

www.judysorumbrown.com
judybrown@aol.com

Nothing's more active than the sea

The roar
of waves,
the breathing
of the surf
upon the sand
replaces the exhaust,
and the exhaustion,
of our lives
in places we have seen
as active,
more developed,
more alive.

Nothing's more active
than the sea,
nor more alive,
it seems to me.
Nothing more finished
than these palms moving
in some unending dance
with island breeze.

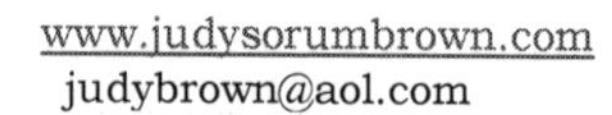
www.judysorumbrown.com
judybrown@aol.com

The hat

The hat
I took
for sun protection
turned out
to be
much more useful
for collecting shells.
This place
is changing me.

www.judysorumbrown.com
judybrown@aol.com

Shards

I picked up
perfect shells
and also
curious shards.
The shards
seem now
more beautiful
to me
than
the perfection.

www.judysorumbrown.com
judybrown@aol.com

Hospitable

Now clouds
have turned
the beach
more comfortable
to me,
a fair-skinned
Northerner.
What we
determine
is hospitable
depends
on who we are.

www.judysorumbrown.com
judybrown@aol.com

Twenty-eight poems

Twenty-eight poems
this morning
before nine.

What do you know?

Obviously,
more
than you
thought.

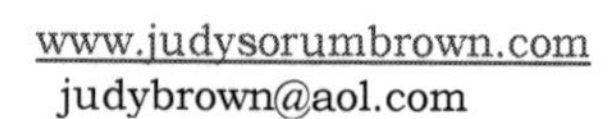

The lessons

The lessons
of this place
are not about
moving here.
They
are about
not
moving.

www.judysorumbrown.com
judybrown@aol.com

The ocean waves

The ocean waves
skitter along
the distant reef,
tumbling playfully,
in an
eternal game
of coral and the sea.

The tide is coming in

The tide is coming in
and sweeps across my feet
as I am walking,
going out
the wave pulls at me,
whispers,
"to the sea".
It's dizzying,
the flow,
first in,
then out,
as if the power
of it turns
my inner gyrascope,
reverses spirit,
heart,
til I am tumbled
playfully in waves and sand,
caught up
in some
eternal game
of "catch me
if you can."

www.judysorumbrown.com
judybrown@aol.com

Why are we led here?

Why are we
led here?
Each of us
washed up
in our own way
upon this vast white beach,
gritty,
glorious,
tumbled, unsure,
aware,
alive,
caught
in the azure waves.

www.judysorumbrown.com
judybrown@aol.com

The shells stand for all things

The shells
stand
for all things,
loves lost,
unexpected treasure,
emptiness
and imperfection,
beauty,
memories,
this moment.

www.judysorumbrown.com
judybrown@aol.com

No one swims alone

No one
swims
alone:
an old rule
in the home
where I
grew up
along the lake.
Safety first.
No one
swims alone,
no matter
what their
strength.
So here, as well,
in azure seas,
for those of us
swimming
through losses
in our lives,
no one should
swim
alone.

www.judysorumbrown.com
judybrown@aol.com

Caught in the downpour

Caught
In the
downpour,
I am
spattered
And
happy.

www.judysorumbrown.com
judybrown@aol.com

The diving

The diving
that has
called me here,
is diving deep
along the reef
within,
the unseen wall
beneath
the surface
where life teems.

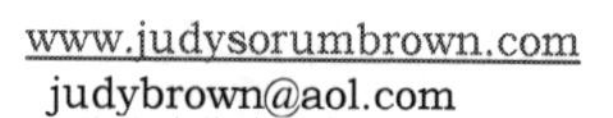
www.judysorumbrown.com
judybrown@aol.com

There is such a place

There is
Such a place
On the earth.
I was sent here
To learn,
Unforgettably,
That what
I longed for
Was reality.

www.judysorumbrown.com
judybrown@aol.com

Some jewels

Some jewels
are of a
different nature--
your calm
and ease,
your generosity—
like diamonds
by the sea.

www.judysorumbrown.com
judybrown@aol.com

I so indulged my feet

I so indulged my feet
In long walks
In the sands
Of Grace Bay
That when
The time came
To go home,
Even my socks
Felt foreign
To me.

www.judysorumbrown.com
judybrown@aol.com

Some places time stands still

Some places
Time
Stands still.
Breakfast
Lasts
All day,
And the
Seasons change
Out on
Grace Bay,
As we are
Talking
And my coffee cools,
And the rains pass
And the sun
Comes out
Again.

www.judysorumbrown.com
judybrown@aol.com

Sleeping by the ocean

Sleeping by the ocean
All those days
Has synchronized
My breathing
To the sea.
I breathe now,
As the surf does,
As does life.
I sense the difference
Everywhere within.
My blood
Moves at a pace
That matches life.
My heart
Has found
Its rhythm once again.

www.judysorumbrown.com
judybrown@aol.com

Sand in the gears

I have
sand
in the
gears
of my life.
A week
on the beach
of Grace Bay
leaves me
now
quite defenseless
against
all the lure
of the sea
and the
joy of my feet
in the sand.
Moving slowly,
I am:
I have sand
in the gears
of my life.

www.judysorumbrown.com
judybrown@aol.com

What is time?

What is time
Anyway,
But a pattern
Of living
Ascribed
By the mind,
To the sea,
To the winds,
To the flow
Of a river
Unknown to the sea,
Unseen by the winds,
Not felt by the river
At all,
As it moves
On its way.

www.judysorumbrown.com
judybrown@aol.com

Clouds on Grace Bay

Storm clouds move by
From right to left
Across the sky
Above the turquoise sea—
Some light,
Some leaden,
Some a mix of both.
And, thus,
Our lives unfold
Before us,
Moving as clouds do,
Across the skies
We cannot choose.

www.judysorumbrown.com
judybrown@aol.com

Before Breakfast

Nineteen poems
Before breakfast.
And I don't even know
The time.
I've taken
Off my watch
And slipped
Into this island's pace—
A natural pace,
Set by the pattern
Of the waves
Upon the sand—
Which is perhaps
Why there
Are nineteen poems,
Twenty now,
And I no longer
Know what
Time it is,
Nor care.

www.judysorumbrown.com
judybrown@aol.com

Elegant Egret

The egret,
Pure white
And elegant,
Came by
Today.
I saw her
Walking
Hesitantly
In the dune grass,
Just behind the hedge,
Lifting
Her right foot
Gracefully
And placing
Long, long talons
Tentatively
In the sand;
Then after
Careful hesitation,
Following suit
With left foot
Just the same--

www.judysorumbrown.com
judybrown@aol.com

Taken
With such
Clear
Elegant
Deliberation,
Each step
Becomes a
Walking
Meditation.

www.judysorumbrown.com
judybrown@aol.com

Dizzy

We hiked
The island beach
In moonlight and
In starlight,
Splashing in the waves.
It made me dizzy,
Turning round and round
Within the surf
In order
To see all the stars
O'erhead,
And feeling
How it feels
To be
That happy.
Dizzy.

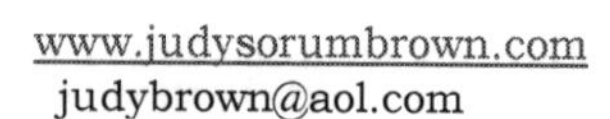
www.judysorumbrown.com
judybrown@aol.com

Different

Nothing
Can be
Repeated,
Even a walk
On the beach.
The sand
Is different
After
Every
Wave.

www.judysorumbrown.com
judybrown@aol.com

So you are coming back?

"So you're coming back?"
You said to me,
After in breezy fashion
I'd talked to your friend
About planning another trip
To paradise.
"I'd come here every
Six weeks
If I could," I say.
"That long?"
was your reply.
You didn't ask me
How long I planned
To stay.

www.judysorumbrown.com
judybrown@aol.com

Sighing

Once, long ago,
When she was little,
She told me
Grownups sighed a lot.
I used to know
The reasons why.
These days
I can't remember.

Expectations

She told me quite excitedly
That she'd discovered
Moving statuary
Down the beach,
Made up of kites.
And so she'd
Thought of me,
Flying my kites
Beside the sea.

The day had been
Quite wonderful she said,
Because in getting lost
And having given up
Her expectations,
She and friend
Found wonderful
Surprises long the way.
I liked the statue of
The kites OK;
But it was
What she said about
The expectations
That I needed most
To know.

www.judysorumbrown.com
judybrown@aol.com

Light a candle

Light a candle
Now and then
To our healing
Of the
Jagged edges
Of this life—
The healing
Often comes
With candlelight.

The moon grows toward fullness

The moon
Grows toward
Fullness;
So we in
Our comprehension
Of the path
Before us.

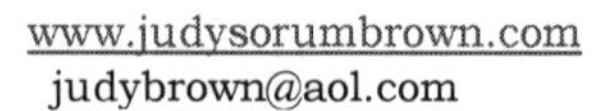
www.judysorumbrown.com
judybrown@aol.com

A bullet train to heart truth

The poetry
Brings knowing
Of its own,
Sometimes deep sadness
And sometimes joy.
It is a bullet train
To heart truth.

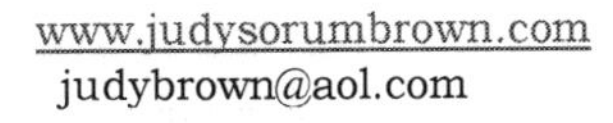

So plant the garden

So plant the garden,
Now, my love,
Beneath the stars
Above Grace Bay—
The seeds of knowing
And not knowing,
Mixed together
In the sandy soil
Of this fine place,
Rich with life's memories.
The harvest's yours,
My friend,
The harvest's yours.

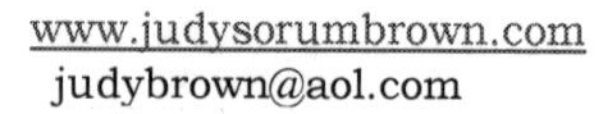

Adam

We bought a bag
Of key limes
And the palm
Outside our window,
Rustling now,
Bears coconuts,
And we pick
Ripened plums
From shrubs out front,
And check the back
Gardens for tiny
Red tomatoes.
This is the
Garden of Eden,
Adam,
And I walk
Barefoot
With you
On its beaches.

www.judysorumbrown.com
judybrown@aol.com

Nothing is rushed

Nothing is rushed.
Nothing moves
Except
At its own
Natural pace,
Even my soul.
Is this
What they meant
When they spoke
Of miracles?

No doom

No doom
At all
Afoot,
Only white
Island sand,
Powderfine,
Beneath
My feet.

www.judysorumbrown.com
judybrown@aol.com

Seaweed

Here we are,
Like the seaweed
Washed up
Upon this island shore,
Time out of time,
No way to know,
Tangled layers
Of our lives,
Stretched out to dry
In island sun,
Now looking back
Where we have walked,
The pattern seems
More beautiful
And seems as if
It stretches
To infinity.

www.judysorumbrown.com
judybrown@aol.com

The River, Time and Tide

Doubling back

Where the river turns,
doubling upon itself,
as it does when meandering
upon a plain,
there, in the outer portion
of the curve that takes us back
where we have come from,
there the deepest water runs,
there the current carries us with ease,
there force of river takes us with it.
So with life.

Where my life turns me back upon myself,
against an opposite that I have held,
back to some place where I have been,
back to something that I had left behind,
back to someone I've known before,
there is the deeper water of the soul,
there the great learning, there the growth.

I should remember this
(yet still I don't)
when I am pulled around some curve
against my will,

www.judysorumbrown.com
judybrown@aol.com

when I am doubling back
while still insisting
that my progress lies
in path that's straight ahead;

I should remember about rivers
when I find to my dismay
that I am headed back
in some direction
near where I have come.
Then I should know,
as with the rivers,
so with life:
the depth is at the turns,
where we are doubling back,
yet once again.

www.judysorumbrown.com
judybrown@aol.com

I made a list

I made a list
years back
of people
in whose presence
I was my best self,
could be completely me,
with whom I served the world
from a full heart.

I don't know
where the thought
of such a list came from.
I just remember taking
out a sheet of white lined paper,
writing at the top,
"Those who draw my best energy",
and sketching out their names,
one at an angle here,
another there.
More than a dozen names.
It was an act of desperation
at a time when I had felt most lost,
at sea within my life,
o'erwhelmed.

www.judysorumbrown.com
judybrown@aol.com

But even thinking
of those folks that day
for just the time it took
to write their names,
I was aware how certain presences
had power to create a space for me
to be myself, and just that thinking
sparked some change
deep, deep within.

Then daily life went on,
and I forgot that I had
made the list,
and many months
after that day, I happened
on the sheet of names,
surprised to realize
that all those folks
whose name I'd jotted randomly
had found their way
into my life.
And life had changed.

I had no thought
of how the change
had come about--

www.judysorumbrown.com
judybrown@aol.com

it seemed an inner navigator
had stepped up beside the captain's
spot within my soul, and said,
"Go here." " Not there."
"Turn here." Return this call."
"That's a dead end,"
as if within my life
I had been guided
by a gardner who
plotted and then planted
shrubs that grew
into the labyrinth
which is my life;
The gardener knew where I should go,
knew where the openings were,
and where the walls.
Thus guided I had been.

But maybe there was more
to what had happened
with those names.
It was not just that
some designer knew,
but that in naming
those whose presence
drew me whole,
and wholly me,

www.judysorumbrown.com
judybrown@aol.com

I too created
the design,
a labyrinth
completely mine,
for which that white lined school-girl sheet
held all the map
I needed
to find opening
and for all time.

www.judysorumbrown.com
judybrown@aol.com

Paris by boat

Paris by boat
was gloriously sunny,
then turned cold
under a leaden sky.
We reached the dock
before the storm hit.
There we were, we three,
laughing, caught
by a sudden downpour,
hiding underneath the
awnings at the dock until
the storm had passed.

The brilliant April sun returned,
laughing with us,
and when the rain let up
we ran for cover,
turning to look back
where we had come from.
There we found behind us,
Paris arced by double rainbows.

www.judysorumbrown.com
judybrown@aol.com

A young Parisian woman, stranger,
volunteered to take our picture,
rainbows overhead,
the showers and the glowering
leaden clouds now all behind us.

www.judysorumbrown.com
judybrown@aol.com

Sweet freshness

I learned
something
quite wonderful
in Paris--
how learning
a new place
with one you love--
a child,
a friend,
a lover--
has sweet freshness,
like the air
after a rainstorm,
or the silence
after loving,
or a moment
in a garden
kneeling by the flowers.
Presence.
Freshness.
Life.
All those I found
in Paris.

www.judysorumbrown.com
judybrown@aol.com

The walk

She told me of the time
Caught in turmoil at her desk,
her private side o'erwhelmed,
she left to take a walk.

"I have to go," she said
and walked,
across the island,
Over the hills,
Clear to the shore and back.

Five hours, maybe six,
she walked.
Next day when she returned,
without a comment,
all was well.

She'd learned, she told me,
that sometimes
when things are tangled,
given time,
they free themselves,
when things are sick,
just given time
they heal.

www.judysorumbrown.com
judybrown@aol.com

Abundance

Abundance
is a place
within the
spirit house,
a resting place
where
sweet sufficiency
surpassed
is welcomed home
and gentled to
her sleep,
rocked in
great generous
arms, given
safe harbour,
where enough
is known
at level of the soul.

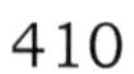

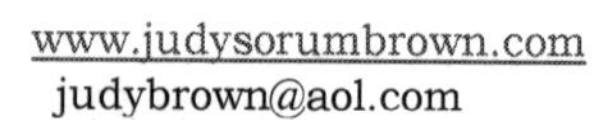

Leadership like symphonies

He said in leadership,
like symphonies,
the stunning luminescent
moments lay in silence at the end,
in waiting, not in rushing in.

I thought of how
that's true
in other things
as well,
in nature,
and in Shakespeare,
in skiing,
and in love.

Such stillness
is a healing
not an absence,
a meeting,
not a missing, vitality and
life found in the silence,
in the ending of
a note.

www.judysorumbrown.com
judybrown@aol.com

Blue roads

(blue roads are the minor roads, side-roads,
drawn in thin blue lines on road maps)

This time
we've passed
has been a kind
of sojourn I
have taken,
a sabbatical,
a trip out on the
blue roads of
my soul,
alone
and in your
presence,
a time of
solitude
and learning,
and of
living
with the losses
that are mine.

It's been a time
of finding, too,
of reading

www.judysorumbrown.com
judybrown@aol.com

in the inner
book of self,
the words of
poetry and pain
and passion,
always there,
and seldom
seen, by me
or those I love.

Blue roads
are hard
to find on
road maps
made by those
for whom the
freeways are the
only way to go.

They're traced more easily
with someone who
can spot their presence
from the corner of the eye,
the pause within a conversation,
that suggests some byway calls to us
out of a private corner of the soul.

www.judysorumbrown.com
judybrown@aol.com

It takes a woodsman's eye,
one who can see
within the way the trees stand,
natural paths the animals
have found and used,
invisible to those who
travel at great speed.

Map-maker you have
been to my sojourn,
a quiet guide to travels
we have taken,
that emerge in conversation
and in pauses, and
then flow as poetry
unbidden and yet
loved, tucked deep
into the map case
that we're filling,
as we travel
blue roads of the soul.

www.judysorumbrown.com
judybrown@aol.com

Current

Currents pull us,
tides, crosswinds.
We come out of an eddy
in a stream, into a
narrow place,
a curve where
water has a
power of its own.

The river has its strength,
the pull of stream downhill
in whitewater, around
a bend, the power of
the seas and oceans, too,
the tides.

And we have choices still
in how we are
within that flow,
as if reed-like we float
so that the current pours
within and through us,
or else in grasping not to go
to some new place,
we lodge crosswise

www.judysorumbrown.com
judybrown@aol.com

and broken against rocks,
safely unmoving and
yet crushed by force
of water pushing against us.

We have a choice,
not of the current,
but of the way
we turn ourselves
within its strength.

We cannot foil the tides
but we can learn the timing
and the grace of turning
so that force of water
gives us strength,
and helps us on our way
to some new place we
didn't mean to go,
yet where we can arrive
in safety, with exhilaration,
gratitude, relief,
still whole and even more ourselves
for having found a way to be
in partnership with currents
we had not anticipated.

www.judysorumbrown.com
judybrown@aol.com

Aching grief

Aching everywhere
within, without,
for touch
and trustable connection.
Grieving that I've given
up that which was
not what I had longed for.
Longing still,
I'm leaving Maine
and feeling achy
for a love
that is my own
and grateful that I
bid adieu
when it was clear
that what I'd found
was heavy,
without heart.

Each year the leaving
is a a wee bit easier.
Last year I drove an hour,
determined,
before tears
forced me to pull off

www.judysorumbrown.com
judybrown@aol.com

by a lake
and give into my grief.
The year before
at dawn I sat
down at the pond's edge
sobbing to the loons.
This year,
I made it all the way
to Portland,
before grief overtook me.
Maybe that's how the
healing comes, slowly,
measured by years
and miles.

www.judysorumbrown.com
judybrown@aol.com

Well of silence

I don't want
to climb up
out of the
well of silence,
up the round
still cool dark
walls of silence,
back up to the
summer heat
of my life.
Here,
way below,
I long to stay.

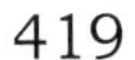

www.judysorumbrown.com
judybrown@aol.com

Circle of silence

We sit within
the circle of silence.

Now the windows open,
now the squirrel
finds her way in,
searching,
now the rounding hum
of voices
bankets us,
now I receive,
no longer fighting,
warding off,
what is around me,
vital and alive,
like skin
that is my own.

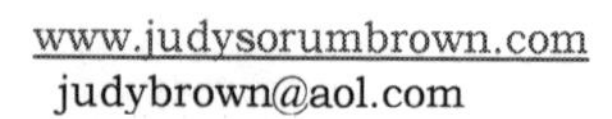
www.judysorumbrown.com
judybrown@aol.com

Thunderclap

That one year
came a single poem
in the summertime,
a voice of power
that I recognized
from far away
as mine,
a single poem
like a thunderclap
before the rain
of poetry that came,
months later,
water to a desert
in my heart,
refreshing me,
making me whole again.

www.judysorumbrown.com
judybrown@aol.com

Now the wind

Now the wind
is blowing up a storm,
the trees
have turned their backs
to us
and shifted
to a sager shade of green,
the wicker rockers
on the grand white porch
are rocking on their own,
as if the ghosts
of early times
inhabit them.

And in the lobby
where the wind
blows through
from west to east,
the sound I'd thought
to be a windchime
turns out to be
the grand old crystal chandelier
a-blowing in the wind.

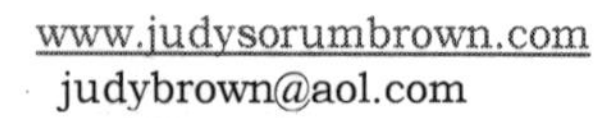

These winds of change
are moving within us
as well--
against our will
or with our
great relief,
it matters not.
They blow through
hallways in our minds,
they change the colors
of our world,
they move things
that seem fixed,
creating music of their own.

www.judysorumbrown.com
judybrown@aol.com

Spirit Guides

Help comes from everywhere.
Minutes ago a humming bird
was near my hair, tasting geraniums
that hang o'erhead in wind-swung pot.
Earlier when I was kayaking
I saw the heron on the rock lift off
and light atop a tree. And when
I drove out to get groceries
a bear lumbered across the road
and then was gone into the swamp
—a big old rambling loose-skinned bear
loping across the road.
Minutes ago the loons cried out,
then after silence spoke again.
The spirit guides are everywhere today.
I wonder what they have to say.

www.judysorumbrown.com
judybrown@aol.com

Our music

He said
our music
looks for us.
That which
is our essential
gift, our work,
hungers for us
as much as we for it.
Our music seeks us
in the stillness,
so he said.

His words
have rested
in my heart;
my task is not
to scramble,
search for something,
but to be still and wait.

www.judysorumbrown.com
judybrown@aol.com

My work is
to create a welcome,
still and silent space
where that which
is my music
can appear
and speak to me
and be heard easily.

www.judysorumbrown.com
judybrown@aol.com

Fortune cookies

I tried to write you
an e-mail, fit
to the technology.
It crumbled into
islands of jottings,
on a blue lined page,
begging to be linked
into some archipelago
of questions and musings.

Our half-finished
conversation, like the
uneaten cookies
still on the table
beside the coffee cups
and my half written notes,
waited when I returned.

My cat opened the
bag of cookies
in the kitchen
and ate them
in my absence,
but she never touched
the ones we left behind,

www.judysorumbrown.com
judybrown@aol.com

intent on conversation
and running for our
separate planes.
Nor did she move
the still unopened
fortune cookies.
So curious,
I opened both of them
when I returned.

One said that you have
everything you need;
the other, you are
embarking on a great adventure.

www.judysorumbrown.com
judybrown@aol.com

Spirit guides II

We hung the food
up high at night
to keep it from
marauding bears--
and to be safe.

We never saw a bear
but we had company
of other kind,
sweet spirit guides,
of other species traveling
as we were,
on their way
to somewhere else.

Some, like the beaver
in the dark below us
on the river, was a sound
and never seen: the fish
that jumped and left a
circle on the water,
the tiny mole that left
us trails of softened earth,
her tunnels as a map
of where she'd been.

www.judysorumbrown.com
judybrown@aol.com

(These poems are like that--
the map of subterranean travel,
as I explore beneath the
surface of my life.)

And others were surprises--
the squirrel that you
plucked exhausted from the river
so she could rest a second
before scrambling out of your canoe
and on her way--
(she made it to the shore)
or that vast herd of deer,
leaping and prancing
as they crossed the river
just downstream of us,
the splashing water of their wake
sparkling like great bouquets of
diamonds tossed into
the autumn sun.

Around each corner
so it seemed,
stood watcher,
great blue heron,
silent as we passed,
or lifting off to fly ahead,

www.judysorumbrown.com
judybrown@aol.com

clearing the way
for our advance.
And sometimes over head
a "V" of great grey geese
called out, saluting us
as they flew on.

They are all spirit guides,
voices of wisdom and
encouragement,
voices of life,
of earth,
of cycles of the sun,
of which we know,
without a word exchanged,
that we are one.

Now that I've learned

Now that I've learned
the lessons
of the river,
days unfold
with grace
and what had
once been fear
of the unknown
is changed
to curiosity
and wonder.

Now that I have seen
spirit guides
along the way
and sat in stillness
well before the dawn,
my days reach out
to me with welcome
and with joy.

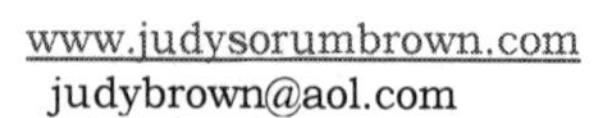
www.judysorumbrown.com
judybrown@aol.com

When we invite each other
on a journey
we can never know
the power of what's
to happen.
It is a gift
that time alone will open,
a surprise.

And when I have said "yes"
to all your generosity,
the gift I've found
has been my heart.

www.judysorumbrown.com
judybrown@aol.com

Tides

In England,
Where she died
At 98, no one gives up
On the small human treatments—
The daily lotion to her legs,
Nutritious meals—
But no one suggests
An amputation either.

Such complex dances,
These are, like the tides:
On charts
It's simple--
High tide and then low.
Here on the creek
Life is much more complex:
Sometimes there is a low, low tide
Where someone's
Emptied out our creek
And just a trickle
Of a stream remains
Within a narrow rut,
And mudflats are the only view;

www.judysorumbrown.com
judybrown@aol.com

At other times high tide is
Most dramatic and
Our big dock
Disappears completely below water
As if some unseen hand
Has reached up
And then dragged it down
Into the murky depths.

The deaths, the passings,
Are like that,
I think.
The papers will report
A simple story,
Of her life
And that she died at 98,
Just as the papers say
On that day high tide
Arrived at noon.
But papers won't report
The detail, the complexity--

That she,
Determined to live out her life at home,
Had managed to do that indeed,
That having gone unconscious--

www.judysorumbrown.com
judybrown@aol.com

With her neighbor cross the way
And her old friend beside her
To encourage her--
She'd taken the one ambulance ride,
That she'd always stubbornly refused,
Through narrow English roads
With snow almost a foot deep,
And within the hours she was gone.
Or that she did
Cross-words far faster than we could
But was housebound
And chair-bound
Month in, month out,
Toward the end.

That detail,
Like the otter walking
On an icy creek-bed,
Is detail that doesn't make it
In the tide tables,
That isn't carried
In the news.

Children don't know a parent

Children don't know
A parent as
Someone who
Lived a full
And varied life—
They have just
Snapshots,
Odd recollections,
Memories of holidays.
It's the story
That her village tells,
The stories told
By little children
Grown up now,
Who used to
Stop by at her house
For sweets, who
Wondered at the
Antique dolls and games.
Those children
Knew her in a way
That we cannot.

www.judysorumbrown.com
judybrown@aol.com

We now hold
Onto photographs
Trying to piece together
Stories of her life,
And understand
Who she would want
To have the dolls.

www.judysorumbrown.com
judybrown@aol.com

Forgiveness II

Forgiveness
Is like downsizing,
Decluttering,
Moving to
Smaller space
Where it's no longer
Possible to hold on
To the detritus of life—
The notions that
We thought defined us,
That we couldn't
Live without,
The views we
Knew as true,
Though painful
And constricting.

All that must go.
There isn't room in life
As it now stands
For all that junk.
I'm cleaning house,
And figuring
Forgiveness follows
From the freedom

www.judysorumbrown.com
judybrown@aol.com

Of new spaciousness
That comes
With letting go
Of all that we've
Held onto
All these years.

www.judysorumbrown.com
judybrown@aol.com

Tundra swans

Yesterday,
When the tundra swans
Arched out of the sky
Like great white
Parentheses, and
With webbed feet
Stretched out before them,
Skated to a stop
In the open water
Out front,
That moment,
Just that moment
Was a miracle.
Like so many others.
No less than
Raising Lazarus
From the dead,
No less than
Our awakening
Each morning
In this place.

www.judysorumbrown.com
judybrown@aol.com

Nature will teach us

Nature
Will teach us
How to be
A Quaker—
In the silence
Of the creek,
Being with
Ripples on the
Water, seeing
Shadows striping
Tree branches,
As large birds
Sail o'erhead
Unseen;
Sometimes
They're swans.
Nature will teach us
Unforgettably
How spirit is
In everything
That moves,
And all that's still.

www.judysorumbrown.com
judybrown@aol.com

Haiti

They say
In Haiti
After the big
Earthquake,
The challenge lay
Not in rebuilding,
But in cleaning
Out the rubble,
Carting away shards
And twisted pieces,
Broken, smashed.
In life, so too,
It's years
Before the rubble,
The debris,
Is cleared away.
When have
I tried to build
Before the
Clearing out
Is done,
Before the rubble's
Gone?

www.judysorumbrown.com
judybrown@aol.com

Seeking the light

The trees
Somehow
Make way
For one another
Over time—
The holly
At the dock
Standing
Bolt upright,
Lanky,
And the
Dancing locust
To its left,
Taller,
Grown into spaces
Left to it,
While just below
Those two,
The one I call
"the river tree"
Is reaching out
Over the water,
Only inches above
Mirrored surface
At high tide,

www.judysorumbrown.com
judybrown@aol.com

Extending like
An arm around an
Unseen child
Who's climbing
Further, further out.
These trees, just these,
Each growing
Into different
Space and planes,
O'er time has
Found enough,
And grown enough,
To offer some
Unique beauty
Solo.
And as a
Trio, too, they've
Found a live
Relationship that
Has emerged not from
Design or
Effort at adjusting
To each other, but
From the process
Of each reaching
Daily toward
The light.

www.judysorumbrown.com
judybrown@aol.com

Tiny bird

Tiny bird
In tree,
Like me
Alone
Early in day
Yet to unfold,
Darting about.
Do you too
Feel the fear
Unnamed
Of life's
Uncertainty,
Or is it
Only welcome
Mystery,
Like that
Of flight,
Sunlight,
And air?

www.judysorumbrown.com
judybrown@aol.com

Secret life

There is a
Secret life
Within this
Tidal creek;
It is a mystery
That teases me
With bubbles rising
To the surface,
Tiny ripples
That appear and
Then evaporate,
Splashes that
Leave a circle
Caused by
Who knows what.
The creek whispers
Its secrets
In a language
That is foreign
And yet
Intriguing.
Listen as I may,
I can't quite
Catch
The words.

www.judysorumbrown.com
judybrown@aol.com

Made in the USA
Columbia, SC
14 April 2023